HARMONOLOGY

An Insider's Guide to Healthy

Relationships Through Music

Stephen O'Connor

For information contact: www.harmonology.mx

Book Design by Zoe Proulx-Lamarche, adapted from diybookformats.com by Derek Murphy.

Cover design by Miguel S. Kilantang Jr.

ISBN: 978-0-692-33642-7

First Edition: November 2014

10 9 8 7 6 5 4 3 2 1

Hi Joan —

great to meet you.

Thanks for reading Hormonology
and for being here for Qi Gong!

[signature]

Contents

Foreword

Music has played an important role in my life for as long as I can remember. I am sure I am not alone in this sentiment as many of you must feel the same way. Who among us cannot visualize his or her life's story to the sound of the important music each has resonated with at various points in time? When we think of the greatest influencers throughout history, many have been music makers. So why does music have such a profound influence on us, our lives, and even the world, and on such a dramatically grand scale? It is because music is a primordial sensory archetype buried deep within our collective unconsciousness—that layer of consciousness lying just beneath our personal unconscious awareness, formed by millions of years of evolution, and common to all people. The psychoanalyst Carl Jung called it the lower stratum of the psyche, the source of instinctive behavior, those which come from the constant repetition of universal emotional experiences, like the rising and setting of the sun, wakefulness and sleep, happiness and sadness, conflict and resolution, and the change of seasons. Music, then, has the ability to touch that deeply unconscious part within us, bringing forth an intense appreciation of the beauty of the universal vibrations to which we all resonate.

What is this universal vibration? The Vedic philosophies call it Om (or Aum), the primordial sound. According to these teachings, Om is the original vibration, leading to all consciousness and

Foreword

material creation that is the known universe. It is considered the manifestation of God in form. In the sacred Hindu text the Bhagavad Gita, Lord Krishna says to Arjuna:

> *"I am the father of this universe, the mother, the support and the grandsire. I am the object of knowledge, the purifier and the syllable om."*

In Judaic and Christian religions, the heaven and earth is said to have been created by the Word of God (Logos). From the first chapter of the Gospel of John:

> *"In the beginning was the Word, and the Word was with God, and the Word was God. He was with God in the beginning. Through him all things were made..."*

Even modern science has identified this universal vibration, this primordial sound, as the "music of creation." Regular patterns in the so called afterglow of creation, astronomers say, were caused by sound shock waves shortly after the Cosmos was born. Scientists have even been able to determine the musical notes associated with these waves. Said Italian astronomer Paolo de Bernardis:

> *"The early Universe is full of sound waves compressing and rarefying matter and light, much like sound waves compress and rarefy air inside a flute or trumpet. For the first time the new data show clearly the harmonics of these waves."*

Music is thus the archetype of all creation to human beings, and as such represents the most elemental feelings of beauty that reside within us. I would even go as far to say that all living things resonate to sound vibrations, and modern science continues to amass evidence in support of this notion.

So while music as a reflection of the primordial sound may connect us to all living things, another human attribute separates us from every other species: The ability to use models or symbols to expand our reality. Tool making is one such application of modeling, which actually helped separate our early ancestors from similar species that continued to cling to trees. In fact, tool making was one of a handful of skills that rapidly progressed our evolution into the world-dominating species we are today. And our persistent use of models and symbols over several millennia has led to technological advances that have ultimately resulted in the construction of massive civilizations, instantaneous transplanetary communications, and regular exploration of outer space and the cosmos, along with a myriad of other marvels.

We have mastered this use of symbolism to expand our reality. Much of the advanced scientific thinking of today has started out initially as a model, theoretical at first, but after some observation and testing, the model is accepted or rejected as a reasonable representation of nature. What is Interesting is that we tend to look to nature itself to come up with ideas on how other aspects of it might operate. Call it an understanding we humans have—whether innate or via thousands of years of experience—that we find within nature a number of processes which repeat themselves. By simply looking at the histories of aviation, biotechnology, artificial intelligence and even warfare throughout the ages, we can see how nature has been the greatest influencer on human innovation. It is this ability to describe and understand our universe from the physical, to the mental, to the experiential, by creating models based on known natural processes that have expanded our thinking, and our reality, to where they stand today.

These two themes—the universality of music as a connector to the primordial sound of creation, and the uniquely human trait of using models and symbols to expand our reality—are what have captivated me most by the literary and philosophical work in front of you now. *Harmonology: An Insider's Guide to Healthy Relationships Through Music* came to my desk by means of a request from the work's author, Stephen O'Connor, to take a look at the book

Foreword

and possibly write a foreword. The author and I had met back in 2012 when, through a serendipitous bit of synchronicity, our paths crossed in the virtual universe, specifically the dimension of social media. I speak of our meeting as synchronous because, having read and reviewed his first book, *Counterpoint to Reality*, I became acutely aware that he and I had been destined to meet. And I paradoxically refer to our meeting as serendipitous because—as I sit here having just finished his current work—I feel a sense of gratitude for the great insights that I have received from the philosophy and model that is *Harmonology*.

Through this book, and the insights contained within the *Harmonology* model, I am able to see that my day-to-day interactions, my relationships, and my work are all a part of a grand universal symphony, of which my experiences are the individual notes and harmonies that make up the musical masterpiece of my life. By studying this manuscript, the reader will see, as I have, the inherent order in his or her relationships—both romantic and otherwise—through the model of the 12 note musical scale. The author has brilliantly made the connection between the primordial sound and how people vibrate individually, as well as with one another, and has created a reasonable model, through observation and research (albeit small at this time), which seems to support the principles of consonance and dissonance inherent in the rules of Counterpoint (the relationship between musical sounds that are interdependent harmonically yet independent in rhythm and contour).

It is twice now that I have been taken by surprise by the author's work. When starting his first book, *Counterpoint to Reality*, my initial thought was that I would not care for the work in its entirety. To my pleasant surprise, it turned out, I was dreadfully wrong. The work proved to be a philosophical gem, one with hordes of wisdom and outright entertainment. Similarly, yet completely unconscious to me, I felt the same skepticism early on when reading *Harmonology*. While it appeared to be a clever concept, it could not possibly be valid in its premise, and I was looking forward to proving it wrong with my own relationship experiences. *Hah!* For example, my ex-wife and I, who had just recently been through a vicious knock-down-drag-out divorce, share the same birth month—a Unison interval according to the theory, or what should have been the ultimate harmony. He was dead wrong here, and my ex and I were living proof of it.

But as I dutifully read through the pages, I could see that the author had actually thought out his model expansively, and as it turns out, *Harmonology* was eerily accurate in describing my former marriage *and* its subsequent dissolution. Okay, coincidence I thought—so next I checked on my current relationship: *A dreaded flat 5th!* Impossible! This was supposed to be a domineering interplay, but I could perceive no display of such by either partner, let alone a one-sided supremacy. Here he *had* to be wrong—this was obvious to me. But wait, lo-and-behold I came across the explanation that people who sit on the cusp of any month can, and often do, exhibit the notes of the month most closely adjacent to it. *Aha!* With that in mind I rechecked, and here I found a strong, stable and supportive 5th interval, hmmmm… As I read that category, I could see more of elements of the relationship I was really experiencing being revealed, the ones which I have been feeling vibrationally, and I thought, "Okay maybe he is onto something here."

However, it was not until I checked my family relationships—to my daughters, my parents, my siblings, and my former in-laws—that I finally became convinced. I could see the harmonious and inharmonious dynamics as they played out according to the diatonic scales. Some notes worked beautifully together, while others, like mine and my former mother-in-laws—a tense 7th interval—were like adding oil to water. *Harmonology* was accurate in predicting which of my relationships were harmonious and which ones were not. Finally, once I tested my family's interrelations *with one*

Foreword

another, it became clear: *Harmonology* is a reasonably sound model of human dynamics and relationships based on the natural vibrations (primordial) of individuals, which vary according to birth month, and how these vibrations interact or harmonize with others.

This work is by no means ready to be named a scientific theory yet; however, I do believe the author (and research social scientist in my opinion) has something worthy of further investigation here. *Harmonology* is built on a model which has been used successfully in musical composing for centuries, as well as a working hypothesis based on the universal process of wave theory. It uses a primordial element—sound—which is present in even the most ancient realms of the Cosmos, and it mathematically compares ratios of vibrations, and interval distances of these vibrations, to make some logical conclusions. When it comes to useable models which describe the universe, we cannot ask for much more.

But more importantly for you the reader is that the information contained within *Harmonology: An Insider's Guide to Healthy Relationships Through Music*, will give you valuable insights into your current relationships, your life experiences and yourself. Take the time to read each chapter, lest you make the same mistake I almost had: to read only what *appears* to be your relationship interval, without considering any nuances, and then dismissing the book as hogwash when it doesn't seem to add up. Nuances among individuals and within relationships do exist, so it is worth reading *all* the information before jumping to conclusions. Once you read all the preliminary information, feel free to check your most important relationships first. Then check it against family members and past relationships too, and I believe you will find, as I have, that *Harmonology* is fairly accurate in describing your current, past and even *future* relationships. Relationships are life's harmonies and we are the musical notes. *Harmonology: An Insider's Guide to Healthy Relationships Through Music* does an exquisite job of showing you exactly how these notes blend together to make up the symphony of your life. I hope you enjoy it as much as I have.

Dr. Nick Campos
Author of the upcoming novel, *Chasing Angels and Auroras*, and the soon to be released, *Seeking the Self through Meditation*

Preface

Each new generation brings with it new thought. Hidden as seeds within the minds of many, is the next level of discovery, the next Internet, the next global insight. Ideas that we may not currently understand, but that we intuitively know to be true, constantly remake our reality. During the time of Galileo, Tesla, Copernicus and others, the ideas brought forth nearly cost them their lives. Often, it muted their contributions and locked them into obscurity until a later day when their ideas finally gained respect. Nonetheless, these, and many other discoveries, changed how we today view the world in which we live. In many ways, those changes are quite dramatic. The rate and depth of ideas entering the world today are even more revolutionary because they change our way of understanding our personal and collective world. At the core of today's thinking are ideas that stimulate and inspire our imaginations in ways that are nothing short of miraculous.

The key concepts of present thinking teach us that everything is connected on a vibrational level. Quantum Physics proposes the concept that there are at least eleven levels of reality happening at the same time, all interwoven by threads of vibratory connections. This mysterious energy is referred to as the Zero Point Energy Field, an ocean of virtual particles that lies beneath every point in the universe. Some scientists have actually called this energy the Mind of God. The physicist Dr. Michio Kaku suggests "The mind of God we believe is cosmic music, the music of strings resonating through 11 dimensional hyperspace. That is the mind of God." (Kaku, 2012)

The beating of a drum, if done with great tempo, causes pitch to occur which further leads to color and then to temperature and beyond. The higher the rate of vibration, the higher levels of manifestation encountered. Layer placed upon layer of these inter-woven connections create the matrix of our reality, including you and everyone else around you. Everything is vibrational and subject to the laws governing vibrating bodies. Nowhere does that play out more beautifully than in music.

Harmonology is about connecting the accepted and honored rules of counterpoint to our relationships, namely, how two or more notes (vibrating bodies) must act to produce the greatest degree of harmony. My life has not been the same after discovering this concept, and after reading this book, I am betting that yours never will be either!

When I started applying the principles of *Harmonology*, everything fell into place. I seized upon the idea that at the bedrock of our relationships we are made up of vibrations, just as in music. We are, in our essence, just vibrating energies. When you truly grasp this concept, it unlocks the power to interact with the age old concepts of music as set down by some of the finest minds of our past. As abstract as these rules may seem when applied to music, they perfectly describe the various characteristics inherent in our personal relationships.

I have discussed *Harmonology* with hundreds of people in every walk of life, and it has elevated their understanding of their personal relationships as well. The ideas underlying *Harmonology* unlock the power that resides within us all to transform our relation-ships in every imaginable way, and now they are available to those of you reading this book. These ideas and tools are for everyone who wants to transform their experience into something unique and

Preface

powerful. *Harmonology* represents an entirely new paradigm; its principles can literally transform how you see and experience your relationships.

Acknowledgements

I wish to thank my wife Lorraine, for her constant loving encouragement and persistence, without which I may never have started this project. Also, I wish to acknowledge her for her continued application of the principles of *Harmonology,* which aided greatly in our understanding of the profound implications of this system.

I also deeply and humbly thank all those who were subjected to the reading of the manuscript, and for their input and insights. They are, but not limited to: Christina Gussin, Dave Gussin, Dan Gussin, Carol Williams, David Williams, Joe O'Connor, and many others whose names have been lost in the ensuing chaos of creativity.

I wish to thank Mary Holden for her first several edits of the manuscript, and her tremendous amount of encouragement. She was a great inspiration who never lost hope for the realization of my dream.

I wish to thank Zoe Proulx-Lamarche, whose tremendous job of shaping the visual and literary aspects of the manuscript was of vital importance. This book would have never been completed without her meticulous screening, editing and expert guidance.

I wish to thank all those nameless and faceless artists and friends who mentored me during my long music career. Without their subtle, and sometimes not so subtle, nudging I still would have

Acknowledgements

been looking for the "answers" to the many musical enigmas that have led to the writing of this book.

I wish to thank Dave Gussin for inventing the book title *Harmonology*. From his fertile mind sprang forth the focus for my rambling and nebulous creation.

A special thanks goes out to Dr. Nicolas Campos, D.C., author of *The Six Keys to Optimal Health* and *How to Win Friends and Influence People on Twitter*. His generosity in taking the time, making the effort to read my book and write a foreword is overwhelming.

Everyone mentioned here has been amazing, tireless, dedicated, wonderful friends and I will always hold them in the highest regard.

I wish to thank the subtle, yet powerful source of my being, for its neverending inspiration and guidance, not only with this book but also in life in general, as it has so far presented itself.

Introduction

The meeting of two personalities is like the contact of two chemical substances: if there is any reaction, both are transformed

Carl Jung (Modern Man in Search of a Soul)

All people and objects are vibrational. Vibrations obey the laws of physics; and by their nature, are cyclical and belong to an even greater cycle. The birth month cycle is one which humans are each and individually tied, and these cycles are tied to the greater cycle of the seasons, the years, and the epochs and eras. By comparing to, and superimposing the 12 month birth cycle over the 12 note chromatic scale, you can discover some very interesting things.

Does human experience consist of random events, born at random and meaningless moments? Or, are these bodies of energy vibrating and expressing the music of life? Is there a blueprint or schematic that describes how humans are to interact with other kindred souls? Is there a way to gain more understanding as to what seems like the random events and interactions you encounter on a daily basis? This is what you are going to find out. You are going to apply the laws of counterpoint, laws that govern how to

Introduction

harmoniously move through musical situations to your relationships so that you can live to your fullest and happiest expectations.

You will learn how to recognize and reconcile the differences between you and your loved ones, your co-workers, neighbors, children, and your society in general, so that harmony and love flow more freely. You will discover that every birth month, every personality and every interval, as in music, is valid and necessary to produce the great symphony of life that you experience.

Learning to apply the information contained in this book will allow you to quickly assess your relationships and adjust them from your point of view so that they are functional and fundamentally harmonious. You will be able to have a greater understanding as to why your co-worker at the office seems to regularly give you a hard time, while the lady at the supermarket is almost always a joy to talk to or be near. You'll be able to let go of past issues with your parents or friends when you see them in light of your musical relationship; you will be able to repair damaged friendships and create new, more wholesome social connections. And, you'll be able to gracefully change both you and your partner's attitudes by merely adjusting to this new level of understanding—a process I call *inverting*. The more you know yourself and why you are the way you are, the easier it can be to attract a compatible partner, significant other or friendly acquaintance.

At times, due to the attitudes you carry, you can override the tendencies of the intervals and destroy what would usually be harmonious. If you've had a difficult childhood, maybe with abuse or abandonment issues, you could be holding on to these issues and using them to undermine your relationships; nothing, including this book, will be able to help you until the issues are resolved.

This book, however, can be a tremendous help in understanding the source of abuses and allow one to reconcile these differences and neuter their destructive potentials. Then the possibility of a healthy and harmonious life can occur more easily. Knowledge is clarity, clarity is vision, vision becomes proper action and the proper action then becomes life without guilt or compromise.

Is there a reason why we specifically choose a particular person to join us in this journey called life? Do we merely attach ourselves to someone so that we can procreate and then age until we finally turn into that dust and dirt beneath our feet? Or, does our choice of partners throughout life bring us to a new understanding of ourselves, a transmutation that is sparked by being close to someone, yet takes place in our heart and soul? And perhaps most importantly, why do we choose to share our precious and brief lives with whom we do? After all, there are, as of this writing, 7,168,945,678 other people on the planet.

Think about this: what if we could narrow this number of options for partners down to only 12 categories of people? What I am suggesting is that there may only be 12 types of personalities, in addition to the *spiritual astronomy* (also known as astrology), and that all individuals in humanity fit into these 12 types or categories. Wouldn't that make life's decisions much simpler when it comes to consciously considering with whom you'll spend your time?

According to Dr. Carl Jung, at the meeting of any two personalities there will be a transformation and neither of the two will remain the same as they were before they met. For each person, a new and more unique personality will be formed, one which will hold the energy shared in their bonding. It's like two notes on the guitar being played together, being held and allowed to ring out, creating a new and unique texture that fills the atmosphere around it with its energy.

Let's compare it to the 12 individual music notes of the chromatic scale.

Introduction

Each one of us carries an inherently distinctive sound and strength—a note. But, when it's combined with a second note, the two together forms a very palpable character—nuanced and different. For example, when you hear the interval of a 3rd you become happy and feel relaxed and at ease. These two notes offer you a soothing comfort that makes your heart come alive. This interval, although almost considered consonant, is thought of as mildly dissonant.

On the other hand, when you hear a more dissonant interval like a flat 2nd, you get a sense of discord and experience a degree of tension and anxiety. As sometimes discomforting as this experience may seem, you can also recognize that these harsher sound combinations represent emotions that we all have throughout our lives, perhaps during times of stress and loss. So, in actuality, all the different combinations of personalities and musical notes are but representative of our human expression—our moods, desires and deeper emotions.

Throughout this book I will be using the terms *consonant* and *dissonant*. A brief understanding of these two words will help you as you read further. Both words are derived from the Latin root *son*, which means sound. The word *con*, or "with," when added to the root *son* together literally means "with the sound," or *sounding together*. Dissonance, however, is a fairly new word to our vocabulary. It was first used around 1500-1550 and has its origin in Middle English and Old French. It literally means *against the sound*. The dictionary states that it's "harsh and inharmonious". For our purposes, it just means "not in *perfect* or consonant harmony."

Together, these two words describe a world of contrast. We will travel from dissonance or *inharmonious,* to consonance or *sounding with.* Each of these qualities is necessary to produce both beautiful music and rich relationships.

The cycle from unison to octave, from cool to warm, returning to cool again demonstrates the path through dissonance to consonance. This process is like following the months of the year from the darkness of January to the heat and sun of June and July, and finally returning to the distinct colors of fall and coolness of winter. When looked at it in this way, you can see that October, for example, brings a maturity not found in the exuberant months of spring. All of nature has gone through the better part of its cycle and, in the process, brought more depth and richness to the scene.

For the rest of this book, picture an imaginary guitar with only two strings. Both strings are tuned exactly the same and when played in unison the sound is cohesive, vibrant and unified. Imagine these strings as being you and the person with whom you are in a relationship. Now twist one of the tuning pegs so that one string slackens and goes out of tune. Imagine how it feels when *you're* out of tune, depressed or sad. When you detuned one of the strings, everything changed. Now, go the other way and tighten the string. As you tighten a string, you can sense a vibratory tension begin to take place. The two strings begin to sonically separate, at first most disagreeably. But with more tuning—more stretching of the string—you begin to gain a hint of acceptable resolution, an agreeable distance the two notes make from each other, giving birth to the first interval beyond the unison—the flat 2nd, or minor 2nd as it is sometimes called.

As you tune one string continuously higher, you begin to feel the new and different combinations of sounds found between the Root Tone (you) and your evolving partner(s)—intervals that travel from dissonance to consonance and back again. Consider for the

Introduction

moment that *you* are the stable, unchanging tone of one of the two strings. Come along as you detune the other string— possibly represented as your significant other, your life partner, your friend or family member—and learn what music can tell you about who that second person is and what interactive harmony they create by being a part of your life.

Remember, as separate from each other as we all think we are, there is one thing that unites and binds us together, a commonly shared phenomenon called relationships. You have it with your children, your boss, your friend, the cashier at the market, your lover, the kid who mows your lawn and everyone else you come into contact with during your lifetime. Take a look behind the curtain of each of your connections and learn how you and that significant other person weave a tapestry of energy that, in its own way, is the music of the spheres—the sound of the invisible symphony of life.

You will learn about yourself, and in the process you will gain an understanding of how those around you fit and function together, like parts of a cosmic puzzle made of sound/soul vibration and tone. Where you once saw tension you will now sense and be able to use the beauty of dissonance. And, where you once saw joy, you will now feel and maybe appreciate the richness of harmonious interplay in your relationships.

Ancient History

The universe, believe it or not, is nothing other than a giant musical instrument with a very special but predictable pattern of harmonically related oscillations, which determine the structure of everything from galactic clusters to subatomic particles

Ray Tomes (Cycles in the Universe)

Over 20,000 years ago our ancestors sat around in caves marking notches on their sticks to represent the phasing and cycling of the moon from one night or day, and then month, to the next. As we know today the moon makes its appearance and goes through a full cycle once every 28 days or approximately 12 times within a year.

The sharp reader might question 12 times a year since, realistically, there are almost 13 moon cycles in the presently used Gregorian calendar. Prior to the introduction of our modern calendar, however, a year was considered to be 12 moons, or 360 days. We might also note that, over the millennia, our Earth has been slowing its rotation and continues to do so today. By close observation and a bit of patience our cave dweller friends produced a stick with 12 notches with which they could determine the passage of the year. This stick alerted them to the coming seasons, weather changes, planting cycles, animal migration patterns and a host of other useful and lifesaving tidbits.

Somewhere along the way each major culture adopted their own version of this primitive lunar calendar, ridding themselves of the sticks, naming each of the 12 cycles according to their understanding, and attributing various qualities to each.

These 12 cycles into which we were born were contained within the greater darkness and daylight cycles of summer and winter. This larger cycle helped determine the qualities attached to each month. December had the least days of light visible to Earth's northern hemisphere while June had the most. In the northern hemisphere, December was also most often the coldest and June the warmest. Soon the different months began to take on the qualities of the observable attributes of the seasons. From April through September the months were thought to be more bright and positive while the remaining months, October through March, were colder and recessive. Coincidentally, this is very similar to the various stages of the moon itself. These cycles operate in a reverse pattern south of the Equator.

About 18,000 years later a Greek scholar named Pythagoras came on the scene and, for the first time, considered the 12 notes of the music scale. Without question, one of the world's most celebrated mathematicians, numerologists and philosophers, Pythagoras gave much to humanity in the sixth century B.C. His most recognized contribution to society and the one we are most familiar with was his mathematical theorem: the square of the hypotenuse of a right-angled triangle is equal to the sum of the squares of the other two sides. Few people are aware that this same man was considered to be the father of modern numerology *and*, of importance to us, the discoverer of the harmonic overtone series. This brilliantly led to the ultimate creation of the art of counterpoint in classical music, beginning in the late 9th century. From his experiments with sound and mathematics, his paths of discovery have eventually led to today's concepts of quantum physics, the study of cycles and even the understanding of chakras and psychic energy. He found that what determined the *quality* of sound in music was the mathematical ratios between numbers: the measurement of the distance between overtones and notes or intervals. That discovery will be of great importance in our coming study of relationships. Although more of a mathematician than a musician, Pythagoras is now also generally credited with the formation of the diatonic scale. You can see the manifestations of this scale hidden in the cycles of all events and happenings in the universe, as found by Ray Tomes of the Cycles Research Institute. Potentially, this also sheds light on the fundamental structures of our relationships, leading to the awareness of how to create and maintain harmony and avoid discord.

Pythagoras believed that all relations could be reduced to numbers. This generalization stemmed from his observations in music, mathematics and astronomy. He noticed that vibrating strings produce harmonious tones when the ratios of the lengths of the strings were whole numbers, and that those ratios could be extended to other instruments. In fact, Pythagoras made remarkable contributions to the mathematical theory of music. He was a fine musician who played the lyre, and he even used music as a means to help those who were ill. Without a doubt, he fully understood the world of vibrations. In the Mysteries, the lyre was regarded as the secret symbol of the human constitution, the body of the instrument representing the physical form; the strings were the nerves, and the musician the "spirit." Playing upon the nerves, the spirit thus formed the harmonies of normal functioning, which became discords if the nature of man was defiled. In relationships, we have two or more people playing the strings of their collective vibrations, creating at times harmony and at other times discord.

Ancient History

Pythagoras was one of the first to investigate the harmonic overtone series leading to the eventual creation of counterpoint, the study of the mathematical laws relating to the manifestation of consonance and dissonance—a primary component in our study of relationships. Harmony is a state recognized by great philosophers as the immediate prerequisite of beauty; it is what we strive for in most of our healthy and successful relationships. I would define harmony as when a being is acting in accordance to its own natural state of being and following the laws of it's governing vibrations. This harmony creates beauty, positivity and consonance. In relationships, harmony is the most desired of all goals and can only be achieved by conforming to the fundamental laws governing vibrating bodies—namely our bodies. A musical interval is often termed beautiful only when its parts are in harmonious mathematical combinations. Yet, you will learn that all intervals carry the potential to be beautiful, whether mathematically harmonious or not.

Pythagoras reportedly used a series of mathematical equations to formulate what would later be accepted as the chromatic scale. Story has it that one day, while walking past a metal worker hammering at his anvil, Pythagoras became curious as to why each piece of metal, all different lengths, made different sounds when struck. He went back to his laboratory and reconstructed the event only to realize that the size differences, and thus pitch differences, were mathematically related. With a little more calculation he set down our first chromatic, or 12 note, scale. Like the lunar calendar, the chromatic scale has its innate characteristic qualities as well; the sharp keys are brighter and livelier than the flat ones, similar to the brighter and darker months of the year.

Now, more than 2,000 years later, these two ancient discoveries, the lunar calendar and the chromatic scale, make their debut in a new theory: *Harmonology*. *Harmonology* shows how both concepts unite for the unique purpose of shining light on the obvious, subtle and delicate aspects of our human relationships.

This book will give you a different kind of key for self-transformation. With practice you will become much more sensitive to the inherent interplay that relationships require. You will learn how to alchemically transform a challenging partnership, through the recognition and understanding of sound patterns, into one filled with acceptance and love. You will have at your command the tools to create a relationship reality that is less confrontational and one that is less abusive and less threatening.

As you read this book, absorb what you can. Over time, with attention and practice, the skills will come to you and your understanding of this amazing tool will grow. Soon you will be using it on a daily basis, dissolving hard calcified structures or set patterns in relationships that are not serving you best, or in your highest purpose.

Even if you know little or nothing about music or the chromatic scale, don't let that block your path to transformation. You are already well acquainted with the 12 month calendar. This is the first step in comprehending the discussions of music theory that I will guide you through that are ultimately necessary to help enrich your understanding, and therefore your relationships. After all, 20,000 years is a long time ago. Mr. and Mrs. Caveman and Mr. Pythagoras gave much of their time and energy to bring you to this new appreciation of who you are, and who you are in relationship with, and maybe even why.

Science of Counterpoint

Sometimes two people need to step apart and make a space between that each might see the other anew

Robert Brault

When Pythagoras first developed his theory of music and intervals, he used math as his tool. If you remember, Pythagoras returned to his laboratory and recreated the many pitches he heard at the blacksmith's shop. He then calculated the vibrations per second that produced each pitch. To his delight he discovered that the pitches that sounded good together were made of simple mathematical ratios. For example, A (440 vibrations per second) when simply doubled (880 vibrations per second) created the same sound but one octave higher. When he added half the vibration rate, (440 + 220) he produced E, a 5th greater. Simple observation shows the strong mathematical connection between these two notes. By continuing with various rate combinations, Pythagoras was able to find which notes were the closest related, thus the most harmonious in combination. As the higher ratios began to become more complex, they created what he called *dissonance*, or a more distantly related combination.

This is a very important concept to remember. Pythagoras graciously did the homework that now allows you to know who in your life is most harmonious and who is dissonant and which relationships need special attention and understanding. Remember, while applying *Harmonology* to your relationships, there are no "good" or "bad" intervals. They are all necessary for the beautiful music that is life. With that said, let's look at some characteristics of various possible intervals.

First, I want to show you what the intervals look like and the overall mood of each. In the past, there has been a lot of research that looked into how various combinations of notes affected human sensitivity and moods. Once you acquaint yourself with the impact that each interval delivers—the degree of consonance or dissonance—you will be able to evaluate on a much quicker level the role you play in your relationships.

The following chart uses C as the reference tone from which the intervals have been built. Note in particular the emotional description for each musical pairing. These expressions have been formulated and put forward by various authors throughout history. Marco Costa, Pio Enrico Ricci Bitti and Luisa Bonfiglioli first presented the list of expressions in their collective abstract titled, *Psychological Connotations of Harmonic Intervals.* (Costa, Bitti, & Bonfiglioli, 2000) They include comments and descriptions by Galilei (1638), Tartini (1754), Rousseau (1782), Gervasoni (1800), Gianelli (1801), Castiglioni (1959) and Steiner (1975).

Science of Counterpoint

Interval	Notes	Status	Characteristics
Unison	C-C	Perfect Consonance	• Stable • United
Flat 2nd	C-C#/Db	Dissonant	• Volatile • Challenging
2nd	C-D	Dissonant	• Eager • Free
Flat 3rd	C-D#/Eb	Mildly Dissonant	• Languid • Stoic
3rd	C-E	Mildly Dissonant	• Cheerful • Strong
4th	C-F	Consonant	• Open • Light
Flat 5th	C-F#/Gb	Highly Dissonant	• Adversarial • Destructive
5th	C-G	Consonant	• Supportive • Complete
Flat 6th	C-G#/Ab	Mildly Dissonant	• Active • Regimented
6th	C-A	Mildly Dissonant	• Positive • Pleasurable
Flat 7th	C-A#/Bb	Dissonant	• Restrictive • Edgy
7th Interval	C-B	Dissonant	• Anxious • Disruptive

Notice here, when you go down the column labeled Status, how the qualities move from consonant through dissonant and back to consonant, with the flat 5th in the middle of the chart; it is an island of dissonance floating in a sea of consonance.

Each relationship interval offers the opportunity for growth. As you learn the various attributes of each, you'll begin to see the dynamic progression of energy developing and maturing, starting with the unison, moving to the flat 5 and returning back to the octave.

- By spending intimate time in a *unison* relationship, the possibility of cooperation could develop.
- The *flat 2nd* interval offers us a chance to be ultimately individualistic.
- For those needing to remain singular, yet wanting to feel some closeness and connection, there is the interval of the *2nd*
- The *flat 3rd* and *3rd* intervals offer us a space to connect, relax and enjoy.
- For those who want to develop strength and positive power, they are offered the interval relationships of the *4th and 5th*.
- For the people who want to experience what being "King of the Hill" feels like, there is the *flat 5th*.
- The remaining intervals (*flat 6th, 6th, flat 7th, 7th*) are similar versions of the previous intervals, but in a more matured and softened state.

We all vibrate differently with each person expressing and accentuating a different aspect or aspects of the myriad forms of human possibility. In a sense, we are like the various instruments within the classical orchestra—all different, all unique. Some of us are the violins, some the concert bass drum, while others are the powerful brass or the humble, yet happy piccolo. Each voice gives way to lend its unique texture and sonority to comprise that wonderful and rich sound we experience when all the instruments perform together. Any one instrument or character creates a special musical nuance on its own, but when combined with another they take on a special timbre or personality, just as when two future lovers meet for the first time.

All of the great composers knew how to carefully combine the instruments so as to produce the greatest level of beauty, power and emotion. The *Harmonology* of human relationships draws upon those same skills of the masters and applies them in our lives, and thus allows you to skillfully mold and shape your interconnections into ones of the greatest consonant harmonies.

Harmonology Explained

Soul mates are people who bring out the best in you. They are not perfect but are always perfect for you

Unknown

I t is no coincidence that the calendar months and the musical intervals are grouped into 12s. The number 12 can be found in a variety of cultural and literary references throughout history: The 12 *Jvotirlingaas* (a devotional object representing the god Shiva) in Hindu Shivaism; the 12 days of Christmas; the 12 basic hues in the color wheel; the 12 Apostles; King Arthur's Round Table had 12 knights. And, when you superimpose the months of our calendar over the 12 notes in the chromatic scale, a new world of insight opens to you.

Moving to the piano's keyboard, we can see where and how these notes are positioned and their relationship to each other. It works out the same for every note. I arbitrarily chose C due to its familiarity and the ease in which it can be seen since it starts in the center of the piano. The C at the beginning of the keyboard repeats itself at the end of the image, where it becomes the first note of the next octave, and so on up the keyboard. Ultimately, it doesn't matter what note you begin with. As long as the months are aligned to the notes, the same results will be produced.

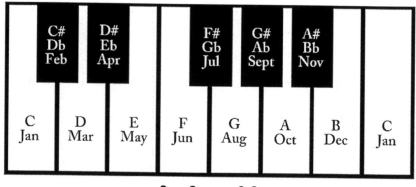

One Octave C-C

Over four hundred years ago, Johann Joseph Fux c. 1660 – 1741, and a group of other curious musicologists (these are the music scientists who open up the notes to see what makes them tick) decided to codify the rules of harmony for all time. Their efforts eventually resulted in an enlightened, intelligent and intuitive system called *counterpoint.* In essence, counterpoint established how any two notes—like our birth months—when combined could create a feeling of various degrees of harmony from consonance to dissonance. To not infer a negative quality to the word *dissonance,* and to distinguish it from the idea of *disharmony*—implying an inability to be beautiful—I used the word *dissonance* only to describe the vibrational intensity of the interval and not to lessen its ability to be beautiful in its own right.

Consonance and dissonance are equally vital and lend to the overall complexity and beauty of both relationships and music. When we think of our own personality combined with another's, we can see that we are creating our own colorful chord or discord, just like in music. Consequently, we all are like the notes on our imaginary two-stringed guitar or the piano keyboard, waiting to be played—some are white, some are black, some are sharp, some are flat, all are beautiful when played in tune.

Determine what musical interval you and your partner create by using the chart below, we will then look into the qualities inherent in those chosen intervals.

First, find the first chronological birth-month in your relationship in the left vertical column. Then, look across the row and find the 2nd chronological month in your relationship. At the bottom of that column you will find your personal relationship interval. You can locate the intervals for other people in your life and investigate the *Harmonology* at play in their relationships: your children, your friends, your co-workers, etc.

Here is an example of how the chart works: I was born in June so I resonate with F and my wife was born in March, she's at D. Since we are working with an enclosed twelve-month calendar, we must place our birth month relationship in the proper sequential order; March comes before June. I locate her birth-month first on the chart and then move to mine on the same row. Then I look down to the bottom and see that together we form a flat 3rd. Now, I can proceed to the chapter on the flat 3rd and learn more about our relationship in terms of its consonant/dissonant vibration.

In the chart, you will find that the primary relationship interval months are highlighted in white, and the inversion interval months (discussed later) are highlighted in grey.

Harmonology Explained

1st Birth Month	2nd Birth Month											
	Jan	Feb	Mar	Apr	May	June	July	Aug	Sept	Oct	Nov	Dec
January	Jan	Feb	Mar	Apr	May	June	July	Aug	Sept	Oct	Nov	Dec
February	Feb	Mar	Apr	May	June	July	Aug	Sept	Oct	Nov	Dec	Jan
March	Mar	Apr	May	June	July	Aug	Sept	Oct	Nov	Dec	Jan	Feb
April	Apr	May	June	July	Aug	Sept	Oct	Nov	Dec	Jan	Feb	Mar
May	May	June	July	Aug	Sept	Oct	Nov	Dec	Jan	Feb	Mar	Apr
June	June	July	Aug	Sept	Oct	Nov	Dec	Jan	Feb	Mar	Apr	May
July	July	Aug	Sept	Oct	Nov	Dec	Jan	Feb	Mar	Apr	May	June
August	Aug	Sept	Oct	Nov	Dec	Jan	Feb	Mar	Apr	May	June	July
September	Sept	Oct	Nov	Dec	Jan	Feb	Mar	Apr	May	June	July	Aug
October	Oct	Nov	Dec	Jan	Feb	Mar	Apr	May	June	July	Aug	Sept
November	Nov	Dec	Jan	Feb	Mar	Apr	May	June	July	Aug	Sept	Oct
December	Dec	Jan	Feb	Mar	Apr	May	June	July	Aug	Sept	Oct	Nov
Interval	Unison	Flat 2nd	2nd	Flat 3rd	3rd	4th	Flat 5th	5th	Flat 6th	6th	Flat 7th	7th

Because the energy between two people is constantly in flux, like throwing a ball (or at times a hot potato) to each other, the dynamics of interpersonal power regularly changes. If you are aware of The I-Ching, or Book of Changes, (Wilhelm, 1967) you know that numbers six and nine are moving numbers—they eventually reverse their polarity and become nine and six, producing a matured difference in meaning and energy. The same thing happens in relationships—at moments you are the driving force and at other moments your partner is leading. It's as if two people, spontaneously and fluidly synchronized, are spiritually dancing together.

This eternal play of energy is expressed in music when either the Root Tone, the one whose birth-month appears first on the calendar, moves up to its octave or the Harmony Tone, the one whose birth-month appears second, moves down an octave. That is called *Inversion.* For example, by moving up the octave, the Root Tone doubles the vibratory rate of their birth month. In music, A880 is the octave of A440, or mathematically double the vibrations per minute. At that point, the Harmony Tone and Root Tone exchange positions.

An example would be the interval of a flat 3rd. Let's go back to the example of my wife and me. In this example, March, or D, is the Root Tone. It determines that the interval is a flat 3rd. When D jumps the octave to the next D higher, the strength of the interval drops onto the shoulders of the F so that our D-F becomes F-D. That movement to the next octave, without actually changing notes, has successfully created the interval of a 6th. Almost every interval has this ability to morph its potential. You will soon see that by changing these polarities you can neutralize many difficult situations or, in some instances, avoid a confrontation, even before it has a chance to blossom. It's like discovering and preventing weeds before they begin growing in your beautiful garden.

Harmonology Explained

The exceptions to this constant changing of energies can be found at the level of unison, where both notes are the same (and when they change octaves they still remain the same) and the flat 5th. With the flat 5th, when they change they also remain the same, but there is often a power struggle involved. An example would be my birth-month (June, F) and my daughter's (December, B). This combination, according to the chart, creates a flat 5th. The F and the B, when inverted by the octave jump, produce B and F—the same flat 5th interval.

For these combinations, there is no way to avoid remaining unison or flat 5th. Both the unison and flat 5th have different needs of which they must be informed in order to soften their impact on each other and those around them. Some relationships need special handling and *Harmonology* has a solution for them.

Some intervals sound good, others can sound harsh or even disturbing to our ears. While they are all good from their own perspective, some intervals deserve special attention. That is where referring to this book comes in handy. By applying what you are reading here, you will be able to knowingly and positively influence your relationship and move it to a more healthy, successful and loving place.

When you closely investigate the many musical interval combinations, you begin to see that they reflect all of our human emotions and desires. When two people interact in a relationship, some develop intimacy, closeness and elect loyalty based on respect. Others opt for friendship instead of an intimate relationship. And still yet, some people crave total empowerment and even domination over their relationship partner. Often you unknowingly chose your relationships to satisfy these inner drives. As you can see, we are complex creatures with complex needs.

Thankfully, the 12 musical intervals beautifully reflect and contain these different personalities—from consonant to dissonant, from nurturing to aloof—that are created from your desires and personal expressions. Within these combinations, there are those that are right for you and those that need to be understood and perhaps avoided. After reading this book, you'll easily be able to recognize these social interplays, and chose the ones in which you wish to consciously participate.

The graph below will help you visualize the intervals and their flow as they move from the perfectly consonant unison on the left, through the dissonance of the flat 2nd through 3rd intervals, to the consonant 4th and to the ultimately dissonant flat 5th in the middle. The flow then inverts and returns to the perfectly consonant octave on the right. This is important to help you gain a feel for the level of intensity of the various intervals.

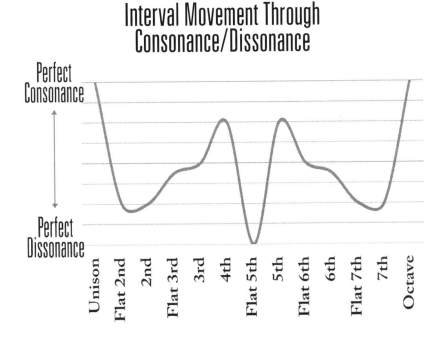

Interval Movement Through Consonance/Dissonance

Research

Generally speaking, the germ of a future composition comes suddenly and unexpectedly...It takes root with extraordinary force and rapidity, shoots up through the earth, puts forth branches and leaves, and finally blossoms

Peter Ilich Tchaikovsky (The Life and Letters of Peter Ilich Tchaikovsky, 1906)

The inspiration for this book presented itself to me one day while I had a conversation with my wife, Lorraine (Lolo). We were casually talking about an issue we both had with a "particular" family member (if you have a "particular" relationship in your family as well, you will know what I mean). When you read the chapter titled Charting Family Dynamics you gain new insight and 'in-hearing' as to why family dynamics often include at least one challenging combination.

In that conversation, Lolo and I threw ideas back and forth as to why this contentious issue always seemed to be present—just under the surface—when we were all together. I asked Lolo what the birth date was for this "particular" person in our family—it was July. I reminded myself that sometimes I have had difficulties with July people. Maybe that was it! I was born in June, and I have often felt a rub, for no observable reason, with some people born a month earlier or later than my birth month.

For some unknown reason, my mind flashed to a piano keyboard. It was then that I saw, in my inner vision, the 12 months of the year superimposed over the 12 notes of the chromatic scale. "Well, of course," I said to my wife. "June and July are a ½ step apart." She looked at me as though I had totally lost all grasp of reality and said: "What has that got to do with our little problem?" To me it was as clear as a beautiful day in Canada when the sun *finally* comes out: all relationships are like musical intervals. They are part of the great harmony of life, filled with *consonance and dissonance!*

This revelation occurred just as my wife and I happened to be observing dissonance at play in our lives. This got me thinking, and then exploring this new theory a bit more. Because I'm not a scientist and do not work in a laboratory, I had to create a makeshift one from the people I could observe who were present in my own social reality.

I charted it out, I spelled it out, and then I applied it first to my relationship with my wife, then my children and then my birth family. Lolo and I both sat stunned from the accuracy of the results; this was taking us into some new thinking that was very exciting.

When I first decided to write this book, I took a set amount of time preparing and asking questions. Most everyone I ran into was offered the chance to be part of my experiment. Soon I had 98 participants eagerly waiting to know what their relationships looked like when *Harmonology* was applied. Everyone wanted to know the nitty-gritty details of the inner-connections (or anti-connections) with their lovers, children, siblings and others. I needed more data so I decided to perform my research with that small list since I had to have firsthand experience with each person to verify the conclusions. I promised myself the list would grow as new participants became available, and so it has.

Now that you are reading this book, I urge you to do your own unofficial science project with *Harmonology*. At the end of this book I provide my contact information so that you are able to report your results and ideas to me. The more research I gather, the more my theory is able to grow, and the more it grows the more it is able to offer insights and comfort to those who are seeking a better personal world.

As I expanded the number of participants, very exciting things began to show. I have included a table of my findings from the survey in the Appendix. Curiously, I found that the results of this survey indicate certain intervals are not as commonly formed as others.

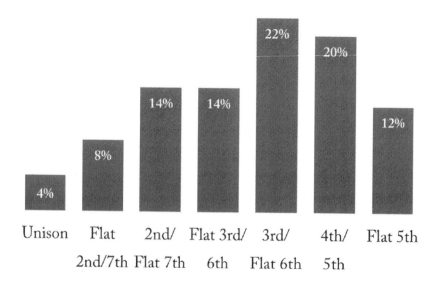

Percent of Interval Relationships From Survey

What's exciting here is that of the 49 couples surveyed, the bulk of the participants fall into the 3rd/flat 6th (22%) and the consonant 4th/5th (20%) interval relationships. The fewest long-term relationships fall into the consonant unison/octave (4%) and the flat 2nd/7th (8%) intervals.

All relationships—consonant or dissonant—have value because each person you relate to teaches you things about yourself you didn't know. Some dissonant relationships may seem to be consonant at first, and vice versa. It would be an interesting investigation, best left to scientific research, to delve into the mental and emotional mechanisms that determine personal attraction or repulsion. Why would you choose to be in an interval-relationship of a flat 2nd or a 3rd? Why do you sometimes crave the more challenging dissonant flat 5th connection over an easier consonant flat 3rd relationship? Do you even consciously sense the unseen draw that a total stranger has to you?

I interviewed one young lady for this book who has had a very difficult time maintaining a nurturing adult relationship with a man. Her interval with her mother was a flat 3rd. They got along well and functioned together with ease. She created a 3rd interval with her father, but he carried some baggage around control issues that caused for a stormy relationship for the two of them.

Most of this young lady's romantic partners have been, like her father, over-controlling. Perhaps unconsciously, she has chosen relationships with men in either the flat 3rd or 3rd interval. This woman is repeatedly attempting to reproduce her paternal family interval patterns with her partners, complete with her father's control-issue baggage. The interval of the flat 3rd and 3rd that she continuously seeks out to reproduce in her personal love life is too reminiscent of the childhood dynamics she experienced. *Harmonology* can help her pay attention to this pattern. The pattern needs to be broken.

Research

For her situation, I would recommend that she look for someone born in a month that forms either unison, 4th or 5th interval relationship with her birth month. By doing so, she would break that habitual chain of design inherited from her immediate family. The unison would provide her with a soul mate instead of a father image. Or, a 4th and 5th interval relationship would help create a stronger, more grounded version of the unison interval relationship. In an interval relationship of a 4th or 5th, she would have strong support plus plenty of space in which to function as an individual. Normally, the flat 3rd would have been great. But, since it reproduced the original and undesired family dynamic, a move to something more open would be of benefit. The potential partners born in complimentary *consonant* birth months to hers (unison, 4th and 5th) would also allow her a greater environment in which to experience freedom and self-empowerment.

That last example was just one of the ways *Harmonology* could be applied to your life. By making a subtle shift in your relationship dynamic, you can attract the quality of interactions you desire and deserve. Use it to take control of your life and help cease the reoccurring spiral of unhealthy relationships you may be experiencing.

You can use the image below to help you determine your degree of consonant to dissonant interval relationships. On a sheet of paper, draw a similar shape (or go to www.harmonology.mx to print blank copies) and place your birth month in the first position on the far left ("Unison"). Then, fill in the remaining months. The image below is formulated for the month of January but any month may be substituted. Let us say you are born in September. Simply draw your own chart with September being the first month ("Unison"), and continue clockwise chronologically around the circle. Your personal chart would be of special interest in planning for a child, understanding a family member, changing a friendship from rocky to smooth or navigating a romance. In some cases, it could help with understanding workplace situations, or perhaps even in the hiring of an employee. Depending on your desires you could possibly pre-establish the degree of harmony you could expect from that new relationship.

Our musicologist friends from the 12th century were way ahead of everyone at that time when they discovered and named the following:

- ✓ *Perfect Consonance:* Unison and octave, 4th and 5th,
- ✓ *Imperfect Consonance:* 3rd and 6th, flat 3rd and flat 6th. These can also be called mildly dissonant
- ✓ *Dissonance:* Flat 2nd and 7th, 2nd and flat 7th, flat 5th

Looking at the image above, you'll see that some combinations of notes create consonance while some form dissonance. For example, our January birth month combined with February or March creates a potentially unstable interval. Likewise, January combined with June or May, is very auspicious and tends toward a brighter and more harmonious relationship. It's also interesting to note that when passing the flat 5th interval on the chart, the remaining intervals are a mirror image of the first half.

Balance

If you hit a wrong note, then make [it] right by what you play afterwards

Joe Pass (Zen Guitar, Sudo)

Much will been written about the attributes of the various intervals. In some cases, the descriptions will seem to be vague or slightly off the mark. When that happens look to see what the birth date is for each person. Often you'll find that one or both persons are born on the cusp of the month, the days immediately preceding or following the birth month. For example, someone born on the 29th or 30th may be "borrowing" the energy and influence of the subsequent month. The outcome of this will show as vacillations between the characteristics of both months. A person born on July 31st in a relationship with someone born in December technically creates a 5th. But, the cusp of July-August (July 31st) can, in essence, change that interval from a 5th to a flat 6th, or even display a little of each. Often, it seems that there is a constant shifting between the divergent energies of those on the cusp, sometimes making it difficult to know exactly where the relationship stands. Similarly, in astrology, the 12 months are listed as "signs." Though they correspond to the calendar months in many ways, the signs often share days, even weeks with their neighboring months. That shared space is called a "cusp." Over the centuries, the dates for those astrological signs, based on the continually shifting position of the constellations, have changed. Therefore, I have chosen to use the calendar months for *Harmonology*. Along with their rigid and locked dates, they present a more simplistic view of our 12 unique energies, though, the cusps still exert their influence.

This gets even more complicated when both people are on the cusp. Great care then needs to be taken to determine where the relationship falls. For people with this complication, it could be challenging, and fun, to try to "figure" this out. More about that could be written in a future book on relationships, a more detailed inspection of the months and using the astrological calendar.

With all that being said, most of our readings will be accurate and suitable for this kind of a study. Overall, the most compelling attribute for reconciling the issues inherent in any given interval is balance. By being in-tune and remaining sensitive to the forces at play, one can then make slight changes in reactions to diffuse or correct a situation that could eventually cause harm or strife between two people. Later, I will discuss *inverting*—a great way to change the energy dynamics when tension arises.

When looking at the flat 2nd interval, you can see that it has an inherent dissonance. Without knowing this, there will most likely be a clash when one or the other party becomes too dominant. However, when this occurs, one only has to deflect the incoming strong energy like a matador with his cape, allowing the bull to attack and pass but not get too close as to cause harm. That is BALANCE: allowing the strong energy to pass by and not let it disrupt your outlook or attitude.

An old friend called while I was writing this book and asked me about her new partner. She was born in April, and he was born in May. I explained that they were forming a flat 2nd interval and then went on to describe what that meant. I told her that it was going to be a highly challenging relationship. I also reassured her that for some people, the flat 2nd is exactly what they want—finding joy and happiness in the seeming chaos and highly energized arena of this connection. I didn't, however, think *that* was what she was looking for at her age. When I offered her that brief synopsis she gave a sigh of recognition and went on to say that her partner was often becoming very domineering, making her feel weakened and defeated. His overpowering behavior was most likely unintentional, but had the effect of regrettably diminishing her precious strengths.

I explained that if she wanted to remain in the relationship she needed to create balance. I suggested that for her to be prepared for his way of approaching life, she would need to be able to acknowledge it and let it go, like the matador with the bull. I suppose that this is a form of spiritual Aikido, but it does have the effect of defusing a situation that potentially could foster damaging resentment in the future. Unfortunately, or not, they soon broke up after we spoke.

Almost every interval can be softened by the use of balance. The only interval that has inherent in its nature an unresolvable dissonant quality is the flat 5th. In that case, one person will always be dominant and the other passive. The push-pull here is more like just push! Some people seek out and thrive in relationships like the flat 5th, all intervals are good if each individual is in agreement and not just trapped in a blind, unrewarding and frustrating experience. Even then, balance will help ease the discomforts of the challenging moments. Learn, by studying this book, to recognize where you stand with your partner, child, parent, neighbor or employer. Then play inside the dance of the universe, the ebb and flow of interactions that make each couple unique.

Inverting

All situations and all people contain beauty, but it is up to us to see it. When we don't see it, our immediate response is to blame, then change the outer thing rather than change our perspective or our octave. It is only when we change octaves that we can see things as they really are. Then, and only then, can we make a positive change when and where it needs to be made.

Victor Wooten (The Music Lesson, 2008)

This book is not based on any scientific research. Instead, it's solely based on my personal search. As far as I know, the subject matter is unique and original. It has never before been espoused upon nor put to any extensive laboratory analysis. What I am about to share are my thoughts alone.

While this study is offered for your benefit to help you evaluate and then adjust your relationships, it ultimately is really about you: how you consciously think, how you sensitively react and how you adapt and evolve while on your personal life journey.

Our current model of reality, thanks to quantum physics, suggests that by our mere participation in life we help form and create our world. As we think, so we become. In relationships it is no different. Yet, often we interact with our loved-ones in an unconscious and automatic manner that reflects the social indoctrination of our times. Whether we acknowledge it or not, we are made up of myriads of borrowed and often unjustified concepts and paradigms. Our parents, our schools and our society constantly and tirelessly placed their unquestioned parameters of reality upon us, creating a solidified and, at times, unsustainable box from which to view the world. Hence, the seeming difficulties we all encounter when being in a close relationship.

It is when we are not loving, stemming from only left-brained thinking, that we hurt one another. When we move to right-brained thinking we have compassion for others. We understand and have empathy for their suffering or wounds. Our hearts are open and we want to be supportive to them. In every interval, that move to the feminine principle (right-brained thinking) or heart-centered being creates the space where love, compassion and understanding can be found. By being sensitive to the interplay you share with another, you will be able to make that interval shift and move a greater distance toward creating a higher level of harmony.

Your relationships are your crucible for personal growth, so really, it is all about you. The level of harmony you create in your life is a result of the choices you make, the thoughts you have and your actions that play out. It's up to you to shape the level of consonance or dissonance you need in your life in order to learn and grow. When issues arise, it's up to either the Root Tone to strengthen their vibration so their partner carries the weight or for the Harmony Tone to release their vibrations and become more grounded, for this transition to happen. This is called *inversion*.

As discussed earlier, an interval-relationship is determined by identifying the distance between the birth months of the two parties involved, using the first chronological month as the starting point. *Inverting*, however, is the process of opening up your interval

Inverting

to a more mature and malleable environment. One example of this process is when the first note, or Root Tone, of the interval jumps up an octave and becomes the second note in the interval. When this jump happens, a greater distance between the notes (months) is created. With that distance comes a space in which to maneuver in order to resolve the tension inherent in that interval. As you read your relationship-intervals, ensure you take the time to read the chapter for your inversion-interval as well. It is imperative for you to understand what you are trying to move towards to provide you with the insight and perspective needed to fully achieve the growth and equilibrium found through *inversion*

For example, if you were born in January (C) and your partner was born in February (Db), creating a flat 2nd (January/February or C/Db), *you* could invert to your higher octave, and instead transform to a 7th interval (February/January or Db/C) when your interactions get tense or too challenging. Or, if your partner observes the tension or that you're stressed requiring additional support, they could invert to a lower octave and become the strength and Root Tone you need to aid you in your time of need. As you'll read, the interval of a flat 2nd is as tight of an operating space as one can get with the two notes being only *one* half step apart. When the C inverts to the next octave it opens up *eleven* half steps between it and its partner, the Db, and both of you now have a much greater spatial arena in which to function. While both intervals are dissonant and contain the same notes as before, the inversion shows a greater promise for reconciliation and mediation.

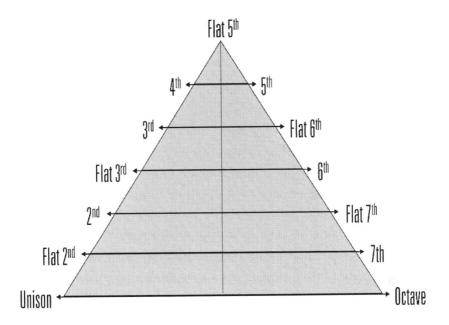

Notice how each of the seven intervals, starting with the unison at the bottom of the image, has its inverted counterpart on the opposite side. You can follow the intervals from the unison, on the left, all the way up passing through the apex, the flat 5th, and down again to the octave. Note how many of the intervals you went through to make that journey. When the intervals *invert* they pass through a similar process, one that leaves them softer and "wiser." In a way, the intervals that develop past the flat 5th and proceed to the octave carry with them a built-in sense of heart thinking. The "left-brained" edginess of the flat 2nd gives way to the softer, more sensitive "right-brained" 7th.

Each and every interval has the ability to *invert* or transcend the often difficult and tight confines inherent in their structure. There is however, the exception of the flat 5th. This interval is the balancing point between the two sets of seven intervals, the apex; it is an interval like no other. Where the former relationships possess the ability to *invert* into a softer and more mature form, the flat 5th lies static at the top of the pyramid without a counterpart and therefor without the ability to invert. It is trapped within its own structure. Instead, the flat 5th has the unique ability to use a technique termed *lateralization* to find the peace and compassion in your relationship-interval, discussed in detail in the chapter on the flat 5th. Though the flat 5th interval is limited to this technique, **all** intervals benefit from the usage of *lateralization*. For this reason, all readers are strongly encouraged to read that section as well.

In a great sense, *inverting* and *lateralization* means moving between our yin/yang polarities. In ancient China, the sunny side of the hill was considered yang while the shady side yin. Qi Gong Master Solala Towler, categorizes yang as brightness, heat, activity, upward and outward direction, aggressiveness, expansion, and what we might think of as maleness. While yin expresses darkness, water, coldness, rest, inward and downward direction, stillness, receptivity, and what we might think of as femaleness.

He further states that we all contain within us qualities of both yin and yang, being two sides of one concept, as in hot/cold, up/down, war/peace, on/off. Towler suggests that we can learn to consciously move between these polarities within ourselves, and, by doing so, employ that shift to better resolve an issue or difficulty we may be encountering. It is the result of shifting our individual yin/yang from passiveness or aggressiveness, hot to cool, outward to inward, or vice versa. It's all about energy, and energy is all about vibrations. (The Tao of Intimacy and Ecstasy, 2014)

In your journeys through *inversion* and *lateralization,* when the time arrives for the polarities to shift, as they will, patience will be greatly rewarded. Calmness and peace of mind are the prerequisites to moving to one's higher octave. As a result, meditation is a key tool to use in achieving the balance and perspective necessary to open yourself up, and make the shift; forcing the change will only cause more heartache, conflict and misery. To assist you in this journey, I have provided several mediations at the end of this book that should open your heart space and allow you to embark on this path with patience and mindfulness, and ultimately achieve balance in your many interpersonal connections.

Unison Interval

Marriage is a relationship. When you make the sacrifice in marriage, you're sacrificing not to each other but to unity in a relationship

Joseph Campbell and Bill D. Moyers, (The Power of Myth, 1988)

Partner Birth Month		Your Birth Month		Partner Birth Month
January	➡	January	➡	January
February	➡	February	➡	February
March	➡	March	➡	March
April	➡	April	➡	April
May	➡	May	➡	May
June	➡	June	➡	June
July	➡	July	➡	July
August	➡	August	➡	August
September	➡	September	➡	September
October	➡	October	➡	October
November	➡	November	➡	November
December	➡	December	➡	December

Staff

Unison Interval

C-C

Perfect Consonance

Characteristics

Emotionally Neutral

Stable

Self-Confident

Strong

United

Focused

Together

Musical References

Veni Creator Spiritus - Himno (Modo VIII) - Coro De Monjes Del Monasterio de Silos/Ismael Fernandez de la Cuesta (Unison Example)

First notes of *Somewhere Over the Rainbow* - by Harold Arlen and sung by Eric Clapton (Octave Example)

Unison Interval

We begin here with our imaginary two-stringed guitar, with both strings in perfect tuning and set to the same pitch. Each note sounds the same and is written on the same space or line on the musical clef. Go to the piano or guitar and play any note individually. That is the sound of the unison. In counterpoint, it is said that as long as two notes mirror each other in all musical attributes and movement they are considered a unison interval. That means that the notes must stay together, be as one, to qualify as unison. They are used primarily for melody playing, but are also often utilized in a counter melody—a second sub-theme—as well. Due to their purity and strength, they are easily recognized and give more importance in the musical structure than the other various intervals. This interval creates a feeling of togetherness, unity, sameness and focus.

Being born in the same month as your partner or close friend is a unison birth month interval. Like in music, both of you are carrying the same incredibly strong and purposeful energy into the relationship. By virtue of being born in the same month, there is a great beauty, power and strength contained in your being together. To be in this relationship is to experience joy and creativity at its fullest. Together, you form the most consonant interval in music. Unisons can go anywhere, do anything, and they add beauty and harmony to every circumstance and event that surrounds them. Somewhere, in the midst of all your loves and relationships, you create this interval with someone else. After all, you most likely form all of the 12 interval relationships within the myriad of interconnections you maintain in your daily life. So, what does it feel like to be unison with someone? Is it like looking in the mirror?

In counterpoint, the unison melody can move freely but also needs to move in logical and easily singable steps to create the most satisfying effects. In your relationships, this correlates to moving and functioning in a somewhat predictable fashion by not jumping to extremes or into shocking and disturbing situations. With that said, the unison relationship has a freedom of expression on a level not found in the other intervals. Throughout the early history of music, the unison, together with a rhythmic pulse, was the only form of musical expression.

The unison relationship is emotionally neutral. It doesn't become affected by the turbulence of those around them; it lives and functions within its own self. Unisons out in society are the most interesting and agile of all the birth month combinations. They are like "two birds of a feather," and everyone delights in their energy. Think of them as the proverbial "Adam and Eve in the garden," before the fall—naïve children. For them, they are the only ones around and they love it and live it fully!

But beware! Those forming the unison can act without consideration of others. Those same naïve children can turn into spoiled brats if they stay too insular and isolated. As with all the intervals, it's imperative to stay open to the surrounding energies of your other friends and associates. Don't be so dependent upon one another that you exclude the rest of the world.

When you look at the unison in music, you quickly recognize it as performing the melody. It dominates and takes control of the surrounding harmony—which at times seems to be supporting the unison's wonderful flights of fancy. Being the melody, it is the focus of the song or composition that everyone remembers. Think of the unison relationship in terms of your favorite music—it knows it's the most important part of the world in which it lives. At times, nothing can stop the flow of the unison; it carves out its own path with clarity and joy and it can seem as though it is almost invincible.

However, when one of the unison partners decides to venture into a new, yet different melody or tuning, without considering their partner in unison, they create two separate and unrelated paths, thus forming the fundamentals of dissonance and, ultimately, two-part harmony.

As you tighten the one string on your imaginary two-stringed guitar, the tension in the air becomes disturbingly palpable. Clearly, you can see that the unison relationship is being destroyed, as the two notes no longer function as a singular event. This is the greatest challenge to this pairing. When the two parts of the unison relationship are no longer in accord, the relationship can quickly dissolve into nothing. What seemed like a match made in heaven could turn into the match made in hell.

Example 1
Jesse and Sally - Unison

I first met Jesse at our cottage in Quebec. He came for a birthday party being held for my wife's son, David. At the time, Jesse was young, single, available, wildly creative, and filled with life. He was living with his blessings, but in a life of solitude.

One day, Jesse came to visit while we were staying in Montreal. He burst into the room wearing one of his own uniquely custom designed outfits made from leather and metal, rings and clips, and announced that he was madly in love! He was more than just in love; he had found someone who was perfect—the very person for whom he had been waiting all his life.

Shortly after, we had the pleasure of meeting Sally. She was indeed beautiful, charming, witty and in many ways his equal. "What a couple," everyone commented.

They seemed perfect for each other. They had the same loves, dreams, passions and pursuits. There was no way we couldn't be overjoyed for Jesse to have met Sally; it seemed at the time to be a perfect match.

After months of hot romance, Sally and Jesse decided to move to the United States so that Sally could further pursue her career. She went first, with Jesse following after he had attended to some unfinished business. They played out their long summer together in Canada before the difficult parting came in the fall when Sally decided that the day had finally come to relocate and begin her new life in her home country.

Not too long after, Jesse made his move to join Sally. He was very excited to see her again and to continue to develop his relationship with her. However, when he finally arrived, he fell into a situation that he was not at all prepared for. During the short time the two were apart, Sally had changed directions in her life, made other choices and went off in pursuit of new dreams that hadn't included Jesse. The relationship ended as quickly as it started, leaving Jesse wondering what had happened.

When we heard the news of their breakup, we were all as surprised as he initially must have been. How could a beautiful flowing love like that end so abruptly? It wasn't until I asked for their birth months that I got insight into understanding the potentials and challenges of their relationship.

I emailed Jesse and asked for the dates of both of their births. At first, when he told me, I was surprised by the answer. They were both born the same month! As I thought more closely, it wasn't so strange after all. A relationship based on births of the same month creates a unison interval, essentially they are the same note.

In music, unisons and octaves create the grandest of melodies. They are big, bold and free. Their purity of tone and intent makes them the prime resource for creative, memorable and melodic lines. As in a relationship like Jesse and Sally's, unisons can do almost anything they dream about.

But, when one of the unison notes decides to stray off and create a different melody, as in Sally's case, the interval is no longer considered unison. Now, it's two distinct melodies, often in contrast to each other. Even more, it's like the detuning of the two guitar strings to a degree that produces a noticeable and disagreeable dissonance. That would not have been an issue if, instead, Jesse and Sally were born in different months. It's likely they would have made a more harmonious coupling had they been a consonant interval relationship, such as a flat 3rd or 4th, that allowed a greater degree of deviation.

For Jesse and Sally, the relationship atrophied when Sally moved away—though that physical move was not the cause of their issue. The culprit of their unbinding was the philosophical and spiritual gap left when Sally moved out of their spiritual *orbit*. Had Jesse and Sally understood how necessary it was to be in sync or to stay united as a unison interval, they could have avoided their disappointing separation. With that knowledge and open communication, they most likely would have been able to function in consort even while being physically separated.

By "being in sync" I mean that both partners needed to keep their mutual dreams alive and their goals in sight even though they were physically separating for a short time. Unisons demand that one person's melody must be the other's, and vice versa—a shared worldview. They need to sing the same song, in the same place and time. That does not mean, however, that they lose their unique individual identity to the other. They each can, and must, put their creative twist on the melody of their relationship, but it needs to go in a mutual and agreeable direction. And to be in unison, the notes must play close together, for if they drift, the unity of sound and the unity of relationship shifts.

No other interval has this primary issue confronting it. Only relationships of those born in the same month face this unique challenge. Once understood, both parties can be as creative as desired in the relationship. They each can sing their hearts out in joy and happiness as long as they both are in mutual resonance and proximity.

In music, unisons can be very playful. One note can hold its position while the other note embellishes their line with flourish and flair, then the two can rush together to go on to new territory and discover even greater opportunities for singing life's song. Like two flutes in a concerto, or two vocalists singing a love ballad, the combinations are endless, provided they are always moving toward the same goal—the same melodic and spiritual resolution.

Unisons are fortunate to work well together in most, if not all, endeavors: in business, as lovers or friends, parent and child. Their bonds are strong and enduring. Circumstances that would challenge unisons are ones that, by their nature, are in opposition or create distance that disturbs the function of the notes to play in unity. For example, vast religious differences, strongly held opposing political viewpoints, a partnership overshadowed by dominance or submissiveness.

Unison Interval

One particular couple I know, but not included in my research, were unison. They had been married for over 30 years, and were ex-Canadian Police officers. They travelled together, walked together, played and laughed together. They gave proof that unison relationships can be strong, successful and vibrant. They were fortunate in that they shared the same profession. For other interval relationships, the close proximity of sharing the same profession may prove to be too much but, for the unison, it works great.

As in the concert orchestra, unison can be found between like instruments: two flutes, two vocalists, two French horns. But, it is often comprised of opposing sonorities–a cello and a French horn, a violin section and a flute, or even a vocalist and a jazz bass performing the same improvised melody line. Similarly, we can find it in many combinations of people–male and female, two men or women, a group of friends born in the same month. Now, just imagine what it would sound like if a choir of vocalists were performing in unison and one person loses his or her place and sings something different, or one person is out of tune with the others. This happens often and, when it does, everyone knows!

The unisons need to be very aware of the close spiritual bond that unites them as one and then continuously respect that union. With that connection in place, there is nothing that will stop them. That is what I call BALANCE—being *aware* of the pending challenges and making the appropriate corrections at the right time.

In summary, unisons are like two peas in a pod. A strong spiritual connection between them is of prime importance while they go off into their own worlds—separate, yet together. When they do begin to divide into distinctly different vibrations, they must immediately re-harmonize with each other. They are a pure, consonant interval and carry a singular power.

Inversion to the Octave

The unison interval-relationship is unique. When it inverts, rather than form a new interval, the notes remain the same but with an entire octave separating them. You can play a C and the next octave C to hear this interval. When compared to the unison, the interval of the octave sounds similar yet more expansive, primarily due to the distance created by the octave jump. As a result, there is no specific chapter related to the octave. One cannot be in a unison *or* an octave relationship, rather one is in a unison relationship with the possibility of expansion to the octave.

More powerful than the unison, the octave carries a weight that demands attention. In music, the octave is used to create a feeling of unified strength. It contains a powerful concentrated focus and gives the melody an even more distinctive sound. Between two people, it is what offers the success and longevity of the relationship.

When the unison interval relationship inverts, room is opened up to support the more freely expressed avenues each individual may choose to pursue. If you recall the story of Jesse and Sally, their unison relationship didn't survive long enough to allow the octave jump. If it had, they easily might have found more common ground with which to resolve their somewhat divergent paths.

Example 2
Helena and Rob - Unison

I have known Helena and Rob for over eight years. We first met in San Miguel de Allende, Mexico, when they were preparing for a driving excursion into the war-torn country of Guatemala. We took an immediate liking to each other and spent long hours discussing the perils of their upcoming adventure. Over the next few years, our paths crossed many times and allowed us to develop a close and warm relationship.

Both Helena and Rob were born in the same months forming a unison/octave relationship. Their marriage has successfully lasted for many years and brought them a level of joy and independence that is often elusive to the other interval relationships. From the start, they seemed to have intuitively sensed the requirements of the unison interval and together were always collectively involved in their daily affairs. Beyond simply being aware of the demands that same birth month intervals make, Helena and Rob intuitively knew how to invert to the octave and continually functioned on that level.

Unlike the unison, the octave is not tossed about in a sea of contentious togetherness. Whereas for Jesse and Sally that matter of togetherness was what caused the termination of their friendship. Had they been able to make the octave jump, with time, they would have likely survived the slight deviation Sally presented.

Currently, Rob is experiencing a significant health challenge. Only time will tell if that becomes the "broken string on the imaginary guitar" and threatens their relationship. My guess is, in their hands, the octave provides the space needed to handle and negotiate the serious threat that Rob's issue presents. Until one of them no longer is capable of significantly relating, their unison/octave relationship will stand the test of time. They have found the balance I have discussed often in this book.

Flat 2ⁿᵈ Interval

All sounds are produced by vibrating bodies, which send out waves

Leonard Bernstein (The Unanswered Questions: Six Talks at Harvard, 1976)

Partner Birth Month		Your Birth Month		Partner Birth Month
		January	➡	February
January	➡	February	➡	March
February	➡	March	➡	April
March	➡	April	➡	May
April	➡	May	➡	June
May	➡	June	➡	July
June	➡	July	➡	August
July	➡	August	➡	September
August	➡	September	➡	October
September	➡	October	➡	November
October	➡	November	➡	December
November	➡	December		

Staff	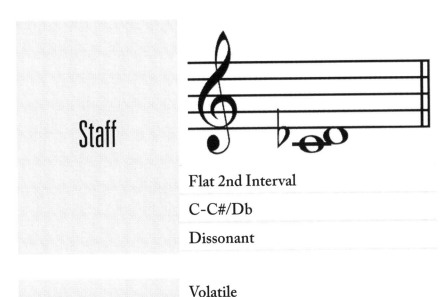

Flat 2nd Interval

C-C#/Db

Dissonant

Characteristics	Volatile
	Challenging
	Sensuous
	Explosive
	Hyper-Aware
	Spiritless
	Physically Exciting

Musical References	*The Rites of Spring* - Igor Stravinsky
	"Main Theme" *Jaws* - John Williams. Boston Pops Orchestra at Tanglewood

In the chart above where the middle column shows your birth month you can see the possible combinations that produce a flat 2nd relationship. Simply explained, the flat 2nd relationship is the one you have with people who were born the month after you. You can hear this interval by playing B and C on the piano or guitar.

Now, let's tighten one string on that imaginary guitar. Let's go a little farther past that out of tune and irritable point where the vibrations are strong, until you hear the first interval after the unison, the flat 2nd. It's still firm, but a welcome relief from the dissonance of merely being out of tune.

When you move past the unison you come to the first actual interval made up of two distinctly different notes. The flat 2nd is in the range of what is called dissonant, with the following characteristics: volatile, sensuous, challenging, physically exciting, and explosive.

This interval is one of the most dissonant of all the intervals. As you remember, Pythagoras was the one who first plotted out the intervals by using mathematical ratios. He maintained that the most harmonious intervals were ones with the simplest ratios—unison, 5th, 4th and octave. When you look at the ratio for the flat 2nd, it's the farthest interval as seen on the image below. It shows the natural overtone series produced by sounding one primary tone, in this case C. As the chart proceeds to the right, the mathematical ratios of the first note to its following notes become vastly more complex and more musically dissonant. The overtone series was arranged by nature in a pre-ordained order and ruled by universal physical laws. Our interest here is in the C, under the number 1 at the far left side, and the B, under the number 15 at the far right hand side.

The Overtone Series

Let's look at the combination of C and B, for our flat 2nd example. Notice that the first note of the scale C (#1)—called the fundamental—is fifteen steps away from the B (#15). That's a ratio of 16/15, a complex ratio and thus, considered highly dissonant. The simpler ratios of the 5th and 4th, in contrast, are 3/2 and 4/3 respectively.

It wasn't until near the 20th Century that classical composers felt comfortable enough to make free use of the flat 2nd when writing music, and that was definitely considered dissonant! In 1913, Igor Stravinsky took the half step dissonant interval to celebrated heights when he premiered his ballet "The Rite of Spring," causing a music world uproar, complete with a theatre riot, due to the harshness of this interval. Igor even went so far as to stack adjacent flat 2nd intervals on top of each other producing the full benefit of this dissonance. It has been said, due to the ensuing chaos caused by his writing that he had to escape the premiere of the ballet by unconventional means, climbing out the bathroom window followed in hot pursuit by the angry audience! This reminds me of a scene from the 1931 movie "Frankenstein." So, if you are in a flat 2nd relationship you are in dissonant company! Just be prepared to climb out the bathroom window when things get rough, just like what Mr. Stravinsky did.

Flat 2ⁿᵈ Interval

The psychological profile for this interval is spiritless. This may seem harsh, but this particular interval is one of the most dissonant of all the possible combinations. Go to a piano and sound a B and C together. The texture is harsh, stabbing and unquestionably irritating. The flat 2ⁿᵈ creates a feeling of tension, unease and expectancy. For a moment, listen to the introduction phrases from the score to the movie "Jaws," written by John Williams. Those two epic notes, one half step apart spell danger in whatever language you may speak.

Those in a flat 2ⁿᵈ relationship can expect a bumpy ride, however, remember there are no bad intervals. They are all needed to create beautiful compositions but, in counterpoint, some intervals are much more challenging to resolve than others. Such is the case for the flat 2ⁿᵈ. The rub between the two notes is palpable. It is as though friction is just beneath the surface at all times. Often the harsh dissonance can be used to great effect when combined with one or two other notes, as in the minor 9ᵗʰ chord. By taking the original B and C flat 2ⁿᵈ interval and adding an E below and a G above you can create a beautiful inversion of a A minor 9ᵗʰ chord. Likewise, by inverting the bottom note to its octave (B1 to B2) and adding an E in between the C and B you soften the discord sufficiently to form a C major 7ᵗʰ chord that has quite a charming sonority.

The lesson here is that the interval needs quite a bit of attention to nullify its overall dissonance and save it from its own destruction. When the relationship is between a parent and a child, care must be taken to ensure the parent does not over control the child. The flat 2ⁿᵈ parent could be overbearing throughout the child's formative years, fostering a deep resentment in the child that will play out in the teen years and beyond. In this case, the dissonance between the parent and the child must be held in balance so as to allow the child fully to experience a healthy and happy youth. The child, on the other hand, will need to be strong and self-determined in order to successfully navigate the first few decades of their life at home.

Looking at the relationship of the flat 2nd, you'll see two people born only one month apart. As with musical theory, this personal combination is difficult to resolve. No particular interval is bad in and of itself but, there are challenges inherent in this combination. Musically it has no sense of gravity, meaning it is fairly immobile. What that further tells us is that the flat 2nd does not want to resolve, it does not want to relax its dissonance.

Two people under the influence of this interval have a potential for continued challenge and strife. We all choose our relationships for the inherent energy they provide; that being said, there are those who thrive under this condition. Strife may make them stronger or more focused and it may be what they individually need to blossom and grow in this lifetime.

Clearly, from the point of view of this study, the lower note of the pairing often must move to the higher octave so as to diffuse some of the underlying tension. Flat 2nds crave to work, and often play, separately. The connection that holds them together is seemingly hidden beneath the surface of their outer lives. They do not need each other to justify their existence; each is whole unto themselves. The chances that they would be in business together are unlikely as they tread down divergent paths. If you are in this interval relationship, don't expect to be tight with each other. That trait is reserved for the intervals that come later in the scale.

Remember the analogy of the guitar strings being slightly out of tune and creating a noticeable and unnerving vibration? The flat 2nd is the primary result of taking that detuning farther until it creates two unique and separate tones. It's like pulling two magnets apart until they no longer become irresistibly affected by their respective force fields. The energy remaining between the two notes,

Flat 2ⁿᵈ Interval

however, is still very active and potent. There constantly remains a strong push-pull of interaction within this interval. Consequently, there most likely will be, like the magnets, an intense and exciting physical attraction between two people born in successive months. Being so close to another's force field may cause sparks to fly and passion to rise. Exciting times are ahead for the connected flat 2ⁿᵈ duo. It could also mean immediate, yet contentious camaraderie if the relationship is in the workplace or at school.

The intensity of the polarity of a flat 2ⁿᵈ, after the heated romance has subsided, could be challenging. The sparks that flew might also have ignited an uncontrollable fire that threatened to destroy the very structure that supported the relationship. In order to thrive, this interval requires maturity, patience and acceptance. Each partner needs to be sensitive and understanding in order to avoid clashing on a constant basis. Again, as in the unison, BAL-ANCE is the key. Being headstrong, although it may be unavoidable, will only result in friction and competition. It's best to remember that you are both powerful. Therefore, you can easily become agitated by the energy that is in constant play. Hyper-awareness is the keyword for this interval. I know a very dear couple, in their late 80s, who make the argument that this interval, indeed, works and works well, for them.

Example 3
Jack & Ann - Flat 2nd

Jack and Ann have been married for over 60 years! They were born in consecutive months, forming a flat 2nd interval relationship. Their love for each other can be attested to by their amazing number of years together and by observing—if you had the opportunity as I did—the care and attention they provide each other. They are truly beautiful soul mates and life partners. Their lives have been blessed with incredible and talented children as well as challenged by very deep hardships. Yet, their marriage has stood the test of time.

I remember once hearing Jack say, referring to Ann in a voice filled with passion and with a sly smile, "You oughta see her legs!" Jack was 86 years old at the time! Understandably, I was quite taken by his humorous yet warmhearted playfulness. It was obvious that their romance was still as rich and meaningful today as it was when the sparks first flew so many years ago. While doing the research for this book I asked Jack if he would reveal what his initial attraction to Ann was. He paused for a moment, grinned, and then said, "It was physical." Are you surprised? It looked to me like a robust physical love could take two people a long way in life, if there were other elements of the relationship under control.

Out of curiosity and, of course, research for this book, I asked Jack who was in charge—who had the command in their relationship—him or Ann? Jack confided in me that it was mutual. At times, Ann was leading, and at others Jack took the reins. But, by mutual agreement, it was mostly Ann who was the center of their world. They flowed in an excellent yin/yang dance choreographed to the melody of their love for each other. Part of the success of their beautiful relationship could be attributed to the mutual respect they allotted each other.

Additionally, for over 20 of their 60 years together Jack & Ann shared their lives with a cat. They laid heavy focus on their beloved pet and at times he seemed to be the glue that held them together. I couldn't help but wonder what influence Mr. Kitty had on the dynamics of their flat 2nd relationship. Could his energy perhaps somehow soften the dissonance caused by this interval? If you look closely at music, you can find an example of the added note massaging the harshness of this interval in the chord named the Major 7th. (Not to be confused with the interval of the 7th) By the interval addition of a 3rd and 5th, the chord transforms the flat 2nd interval into a rich, yet slightly tense texture.

Regardless, it is the care and attention they gave to the strong energy that flowed between them that showed they were mature enough to handle such a volatile interval.

The flat 2nd, being so firmly bound, creates a strong carnal pull between both parties. The energy created between two people in this relationship can be very volatile and reactive. This interval provides the first opportunity the intervals in the chromatic scale have to become independent. Think of the unison—two notes of the same character—as forming, developing, gaining energy and ultimately bursting forward into opposition—individuation—into the flat 2nd relationship, like the tightening of that one string on the guitar. In this interval, both parts stand in opposing polarity—yin and yang, hot and cold, dark and light. We could tag this interval as primal.

With this newfound tonal independence, the flat 2nd presents unique challenges. Being polarities, there is a strong tendency to stay in opposition. At times, this opposition can be seen as disregard for each other. The independence here is often too distant, challenging the relationship in ways that almost no other interval exhibits. Great care needs to be continually taken to make the effort to shift the energies back and forth, sharing the responsibilities and giving up the constant desire for control. Don't plan, however, to do things together very often. That's not in the cards for this relationship.

The flat 2nd interval, has much in common with the flat 5th. It's as though the flat 2nd was the love child of the challenging flat 5th interval. In both cases, one of the parties involved will be stronger and more willful than the other. Seldom will both people be equal. It's best that it is allowed and encouraged, by doing so; many conflicts and challenges can be avoided. Be gentle, take it easy, and walk lightly in this relationship. It very well could last a lifetime, or die in the attempt. Here is another example highlighting how the flat 2nd can appear disinterested and aloof.

Example 4
Bonnie & Jeff—Flat 2nd

Bonnie and Jeff were together on and off for many years when I met them. She ran her own Spiritual Enlightenment Center, and he was a classical pianist. Both were quite capable at their chosen professions—as well as both being bright, aware and sensitive.

I knew that Bonnie's relationship with Jeff was difficult and fraught with frustration. Learning of her interval with Jeff, and after hearing her story, I felt her experience would bring a lot to the table. It was soon after sending her a request that I learned they were a flat 2nd. Bonnie went on to say that Jeff was always very distant and detached (a trait found often in this interval). He constantly wanted to discuss weighty topics like philosophy while she wanted to cuddle and just be together. Accordingly, there wasn't much room for compromise, and they seemed at odds most of the time.

Bonnie and Jeff's relationship exhibited classic challenging signs of the flat 2nd interval: dominance, inequality and opposition. Remember that all relationship intervals are based on sound resonance, providing that both parties are seeking that particular interplay of energy, whichever they may choose. In Bonnie's case, however, I felt she would have been better served by dating someone from the flat 3rd or 3rd interval, where, most likely, she could enjoy the cuddling and closeness she seeks. One never knows, nor can ever predict what two people need and desire in their hearts. We are all complex creatures and our paradigms and belief systems drive us on in strange ways.

As an aside, during the process of researching my book, I noticed that other than these two couple (Jim/Ann and Bonnie/Jeff) there were only two other couples in the flat 2nd relationship. That's a total of 8 people (or 4 couples) out of 98 participants interviewed! It may be reasonable to conclude that most people prefer a less challenging relationship than the flat 2nd interval.

In summary, the flat 2nd relationship is often a difficult one for those not prepared to adapt. Under the umbrella of togetherness, the two people seek and demand total independence. From an outside view, the relationship could appear to be nonexistent. Often, as we saw with Jack and Ann, it could also be quite the contrary. Relationships of a flat 2nd would make good partners in a type of business that required each one to be somewhere different, doing something related but independent. In a parent/child relationship, great care needs to be exerted to minimize the constant tension. A possibility of disinterest and aloofness by either party may cause the parental relationship to fester. Again, the tough times experienced by the flat 2nd may be exactly what both people desire, either for their growth or some hidden need that drives them to experience the challenge. Reading the chapter on the flat 5th may provide further insight, as it shares many of the same challenges inherent in the flat 2nd, though on a greater scale.

Inversion to the 7th

If you were to play a B and a C (flat 2nd) together on your guitar and I asked you how it sounded, you would likely describe the sound as unpleasant. But, if I take the B up an octave and play the two notes again you probably would say it sounds somewhat pleasing. Same notes, different octave. The high B, combined with the C, creates what is called an interval of a 7th and is a significant factor in making a chord sound pretty. It holds the possibility of moving the coarser flat 2nd vibration into a more agreeable, more controllable and more reconcilable one.

The 7th is the interval where you can change the issues brought on by the overly close flat 2nd, to allow for the spiritual and emotional connection required to build healthy and meaningful relationships. When you are in this interval relationship, you are continually going back and forth between the energy of the flat 2nd and the grace of the 7th. In nature, there always seems to be a resolution available, and this interval is a great example. By using the 7th interval to find a place to be grounded and connect with each other, you are able to maintain your independence and prevent the potential disconnect inherent in the flat 2nd. The inversion to the 7th leads to a more softened, richer space from which to function.

Example 5
Allen & Naomi - Flat 2ⁿᵈ

Allen and Naomi reflect a perfect and functional version of the flat 2nd interval relationship. Though, at times, they are physically together they are in their own respective worlds, miles apart. I've observed them at cocktail parties where Allen would spend the entire time either talking intently to several men, or finely and firmly focused on a beautiful woman. At no time during those social gatherings did he and Naomi unite. During the day, I would often see Allen walking through the plaza on one of his important solo missions, constantly leaving Naomi home alone. Their way of relating, however, worked for them. She spent her time at totally opposite pursuits than he. Yet, they are married now for over thirty years, have several adult children and live in beautiful homes in several countries.

Both Allen and Naomi are what we could call intellectuals. Fortunately, the flat 2nd relationship offers them the immense freedom not found in the other intervals to submerge themselves in their interests. The spiritual distance inherent in this interval offers each person the room to spin out of orbit with each other. The challenge for them, as well as others in this interval, is to not get caught in their heads. The distance between them often is so great, it does not allow a place for them to be grounded. It becomes very easy for each of them to feel no need for the other and live instead in their private mental world. The less they are physically together, the less they are emotionally and spiritually as well. By learning to invert to the 7th, they can maintain their desired individualism while still offering each other the emotional comfort relationships often demand. The inversion helps to open that dense space into a more graceful arena of operation, thereby soothing the pangs of the intensity of this interval.

2ⁿᵈ Interval

Music is a higher revelation than all of wisdom and philosophy

Ludwig van Beethoven

Partner Birth Month		Your Birth Month		Partner Birth Month
		January	➡	March
		February	➡	April
January	➡	March	➡	May
February	➡	April	➡	June
March	➡	May	➡	July
April	➡	June	➡	August
May	➡	July	➡	September
June	➡	August	➡	October
July	➡	September	➡	November
August	➡	October	➡	December
September	➡	November		
October	➡	December		

Staff

2nd Interval

C-D

Dissonant

Characteristics

Suspended

Light

Free

Open

Pleasant

Eager

Expansive

Musical Reference

Opening Theme from *Serenata D'Estate* - George Rochberg

A gain, tighten that second string on our imaginary guitar. Keep going until you reach the next potential chromatic note. From where you started, with the two strings in unison, you have tuned upward and progressed first to the flat 2nd, and now to the 2nd, two notes a whole step apart. If you play C and D together on the piano, you'll hear the interval of a 2nd.

With 2^{nds}, we find two energies that have individuated even further; where each partner clearly has to exert his or her freedom and independence. They may act as a couple while at the same time going off and doing their own thing. Often, they go about their separate lives only to come together at crucial times during the day. "Freedom" is the keyword here. There is often freedom to such a degree that it seems to others as though there is no connection at all. However strange this may seem, it works for many people in the interval of a 2nd. More than that, people looking for this connection crave and seek out others that are sympathetic to their mutual desire and need for freedom.

In music, 2^{nds} are characterized by their tendency to not resolve. By that, I mean that they have no tendency to search out a home base, no desire to find a landing point. They are two notes without a particular mutual direction. They can and do, however, move as independent voices returning to their described home interval only after they have individually accomplished their role in the composition.

When you choose a partner you often subconsciously gravitate to those who will provide the challenge or the comfort you are seeking. These circumstances are necessary for our growth as humans. While the flat 2nd, 2nd and flat 5th are more challenging relationships than the unison, 4th and 5th, there are people out there who crave the challenge and would have nothing to do with the ease and softness of the consonant intervals.

You will often see professional couples in this connection. Two people deeply involved in divergent pursuits, uniting only after a long, hard day at the office. 2^{nds} don't rely upon their partners for fulfillment. Instead, they are singularly insular and complete on their own. That is not to say they cannot be together for long periods of time, quite the contrary. They have the ability to be in the confines of proximity but remain in their own private mental worlds.

In the relationship of the 2nd, when dealing with someone other than your loved one or close partner, it would be best to remember that you both function better independently. Within this close paring, you won't need your partner's permission, and they don't crave yours. That independence could potentially bring difficulties in an employer/employee relationship; it may be difficult to get the permission or consent of the employer at times and there is a substantial chance that they will often be unavailable to you. The support and direction you seek may be elusive, causing tension and miscommunications to arise. In cases like that, inverting to the flat 7th would help open the space needed to at least temporarily resolve the situation. It's very important in these harmonically closer intervals to constantly be sensitive to that tight interplay of energy. Learn when to give in and when to hold firm. Thus, 2nds need to learn to be co-operative and flexible in order to maintain a flow in their relationships, sometimes a difficult thing to do.

In music, 2nds are very non-committal, shying away from the tendency to resolve to another note or establish a home base. A sense of floating and indifference can be obtained by using 2nds in a composition, creating a seemingly empty yet beautiful musical landscape. The contemporary classical composer George Rochberg (1918-2005) utilized 2nds in some of his compositions while at the University of Arizona, to create a wonderful feeling of a vacuous and still desert ecosphere. 2nds create an emotional feeling of lightness, openness and mild dissonance. The same can be said about relationships based on this interval. You can hear the interval of the 2nds as used by Rochberg in the opening theme of his Serenata D'Estate.

Example 6:
Lea & Gunnar - 2^{nds}

My friends Lea & Gunnar are 2nds. I've been fortunate to know them for a number of years. They have been together for the better part of their adult lives while living in the confines of a sailing boat and traveling across the globe. Both are artists, but in two very divergent fields; while one enjoys walking in the woods or drawing up architectural plans for friends, the other is heavily involved in painting and community service. Rarely do they combine their efforts on a mutual project or pursuit—a characteristic trait of the 2nd. Often, from the outside, they look to be in total opposition to each other. Still, there is a palpable joy and love radiating from them when they are together. Other times strong words fly. Yet, somehow, they are both immune to it all, and happily proceed down their life's separate paths. In a sense, their relationship seems to paint a similar haunting and empty landscape, as did George Rochberg's composition.

I once remember hearing Lea take Gunnar to task for forgetting a dinner appointment. Gunnar looked at her and said, "You never told me about it." Lea shot back, "You should have known. Now we are late!"

Gunnar looked at me with a smile, shrugged and then let the whole moment pass as if it never happened. Their two lives, like the notes, float independently of each other without the need of a mutual home base. Even though the conversation sounded like a miscommunication, it was really all about being in the relationship of a 2nd. Lots of freedom and independence since that's how 2^{nds} function.

To make your relationship of a 2nd prosper, don't often expect cooperation, support or total communication from the other party—they mean well, but are in their own world, just as you most likely are. Be prepared to fly solo, which is what the 2nd desires. Know and accept that while you both seem to be distant and remote you are actually functioning in your standard mode. Make a point of coming together more often, touching bases before you each sail off into the complexities of your individual lives, this reassures your partner that you're thinking of him or her.

Example 7:
Joseph & Wendy - 2^{nds}

Another couple I interviewed was a perfect match for the 2nd. Like Lea, Wendy was an artist, though in fabric design. Joseph was an ex-financial planner and retired teacher. The interests and goals they held were very different from each other. She spent her time doing art and talking with her parents, who were living with them; he centered his activities on reading and preparing to write a book. When they did come together, they still maintained a distance from each other.

Their relationship, although seemingly non-connected, was in fact a healthy and loving one. There may have been a chance that if they were of the 3rd or 4th interval they would have felt thwarted in their pursuits and their life styles may have seemed cramped by the closeness inherent in the increasingly consonant intervals. Joseph and Wendy actually functioned well in their relationship. While both were dedicated to their life path, choosing the 2nd interval relationship gave them the space to attend to their visions without feeling overly bound to each other. Wendy and Joseph had an intuitive sense that served them well when making their lifelong commitment.

Inversion to Flat 7th

The inversion to the flat 7th is the first opportunity for the 2nd interval to not be as dramatically affected by the gravitational pull of each birth month. We saw that in the flat 2nd that the push/pull was so strong as to make the two energies verge on the edge of spinning out of control through its built in inner-dynamics. There is an aloofness and often argumentative stance held throughout this 2nd bonding. This interval *loves* independence and it may feel that the chances of being together as partners, lovers, best friend, or comrades is somewhat distant or remote. When this becomes too much of a burden, too intense for comfort, the opportunity to move into a different interval subtly presents itself. In the case of the 2nd, it's the flat 7th interval that opens its portal to us to soften the more edgy characteristics of the dissonant 2nd, to soften the friction of this free-wheeling lifestyle, and to consciously join back together. That is when the inversion to the flat 7th pays off.

The flat 7th has a distinct advantage over the 2nd since there is more space to maneuver. This openness creates room for absorbing the more harsh tendencies of the 2nd, such as aloofness and disregard. By moving into the heart space, through meditation, mindfulness practice or just plain intuition, the inversion automatically occurs. Then, you suddenly find yourself more playful, less anxious and considerably less left-brained and analytical. You will be able to find the maturity in the 2nd relationship and the healthy joy of independence, rather than feeling a severed distance and disconnect from your partnership. When you return from the inversion to the natural state of the 2nd, it will be with a more grounded and thoughtful mindfulness.

The first two intervals after the unison bear the weight and density of dissonance. It can be challenging at times to constantly feel adrift or ungrounded and unconnected. Taking advantage of inverting is almost the same as utilizing a portion of your day for rest, relaxation and sleep. It is in this space where you recharge your incredible battery of energy, your yang chi, so that you can jump back into the race and get "stuff" done. Fear not, when you invert you still are a 2nd interval relationship, only more mature in outlook and more relaxed in presence.

Flat 3rd Interval

When people are not in tune with each other, they add to the dishar-mony of the world

Philip Toshio Sudo (Zen Guitar, 1998)

Partner Birth Month		Your Birth Month		Partner Birth Month
		January	➡	April
		February	➡	May
		March	➡	June
January	➡	April	➡	July
February	➡	May	➡	August
March	➡	June	➡	September
April	➡	July	➡	October
May	➡	August	➡	November
June	➡	September	➡	December
July	➡	October		
August	➡	November		
September	➡	December		

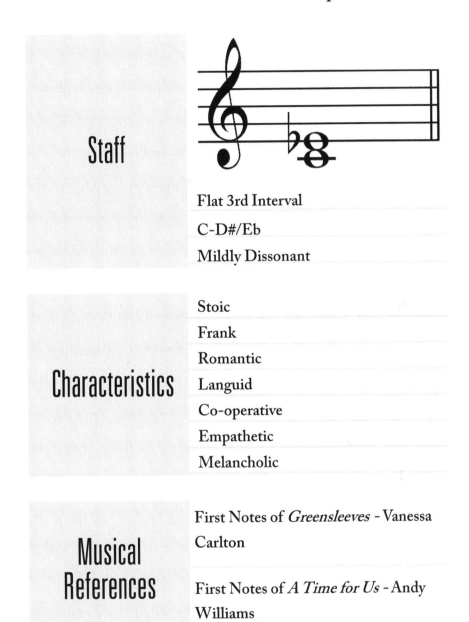

Staff

Flat 3rd Interval

C-D#/Eb

Mildly Dissonant

Characteristics

Stoic

Frank

Romantic

Languid

Co-operative

Empathetic

Melancholic

Musical References

First Notes of *Greensleeves* - Vanessa Carlton

First Notes of *A Time for Us* - Andy Williams

As you grab the imaginary guitar, tighten the one string so it vibrates even higher. From the unison set of notes, you move past the flat 2nd and beyond the 2nd, as you turn the

Flat 3rd Interval

tuning peg until you arrived at the flat 3rd. For the first time, your ears will hear a pleasing and more relaxed sound—you'll finally feel a deep level of comfort and familiarity. This, and the next interval—the 3rd—are the intervals of love. Play this interval on the piano by striking C and Eb together.

Now you're at the interval that contains the first promise of a relationship being easy to manage and enjoy, at least on the surface. The flat 3rd is what the 12th Century music masters called *mildly dissonant*. Today, the flat 3rd is classified as an imperfect consonance and is considered one of the most consonant intervals after the unison, 4th and 5th.

Again, going back to Pythagoras and his mathematical ratios for sound, the flat 3rd falls into the area of more complexity of vibrations—ones of greater mathematical ratios. However, this and the next interval, the 3rd, are close enough mathematically to allow their energy to be resolvable. That means that the degree of balance in the flat 3rd relationship is greater than that of the flat 2nd, flat 5th and 2nd.

People who gravitate toward this interval long for a less challenging relationship as opposed to those found in the previous intervals. With this interval, you find a more romantic and melancholic pairing than those found in the previous chapters.

Flat 3rds in music are found worldwide in songs of love and longing. This interval creates a feeling of dissonance that is uplifting. Think of the call of a sparrow or childhood singsongs. The music of the Latin countries expresses this interval often through forlorn and heartfelt romantic ballads. Some musicologists think that the flat 3rd is commonly used to express sadness in music, and research is showing that we use the same interval when expressing sadness in our speech as well. In 2010, Ferris Jabr wrote an article for Scientific American Online, investigating the correlation between our ability to express sadness and its relationship to the flat

3rd interval (Music and speech share a code for communicating sadness in the minor third, 2010). An article by Jamshed Bharucha and Meagan Curtis in an issue of *Emotion* further suggests the flat 3rd isn't a facet of musical communication alone, quite often, it's how we convey sadness in speech too (The Minor Third Communicates Sadness in Speech, Mirroring Its Use in Music, 2010).

When this interval falls between two soul mates—two lovers—it can be sweet in texture. The two people, like the two notes, willfully, openly, trustingly share their lives with each other; their common bonds are strong and unite them in a close and personal relationship. When we find the flat 3rd among parent/child or employer/employee relationships, quite often they are very congenial and joyful. This connection laughs easily and cares about the feelings of the other.

When issues arise between two people in the flat 3rd relationship they are usually centered on the lack of independence. Often, flat 3rds tend to rely too much upon each other. Since they enjoy doing things together they can lose their uniqueness. Flat 3rds need to find their own unique identity, their own worldview, and then enter into the tight bindings of the flat 3rd relationship.

In counterpoint, the flat 3rd and 3rd interval can move freely in any direction. The only restriction is that they don't move too long or too far in any one direction. Once a pattern is established, the human mind easily perceives repetition, whether in music or motion. When this happens boredom and apathy sets in. In effect, if the flat 3rds stay too tightly together they lose their audience; in essence, they become boring. I know you have seen the classic couple at the theme park wearing the matching Bermuda shorts, shoes and shirts, walking hand in hand. Independence is what must be incorporated to prevent sameness from overtaking the relationship.

Flat 3rd Interval

In a marriage or other close relationship, the overall challenge will be to stay fresh and exciting. Boredom, over time, will most certainly destroy whatever good was created. To preserve the joy in this relationship, keep it new and add the unexpected. Do your own thing but under the umbrella of togetherness. Don't fall into the trap of always agreeing and trying to avoid confrontation. Above all, go out with your own friends once in a while and leave your partner to fend for themselves. Be in a business or undertaking that is independent of the other half of your flat 3rd connection. This will give you all the room needed to enjoy your time with the world and with your partner.

In business or school, or dealing with a neighbor or an old friend who forms a flat 3rd interval with you, the cooperation you give will pay off in success and advancement. Work closely but independently and the results you seek will come. Honor the other person's contributions and efforts like you would your own.

In my research, I have catalogued many couples that form a flat 3rd interval. That seems to be a very popular choice for a close relationship, perhaps due to the ease and joy inherent in that pairing. Most, if not all, expressed a closeness and sense of trust with their partner. Being around a number of these couples has shown me that they seldom carry misunderstanding or animosity toward their partners, unlike the flat 2nd and 2nd intervals. However, if they don't find their own voice and exercise it regularly, and instead live together as one, they both risk 'going down in flames' when one of them becomes uninvolved and bored. A marriage of thirty or forty years may prove to be the crucible or acid test for how well a person can survive sameness. On the other hand, if sameness has gotten a hold on the relationship, change may actually be what takes down the relationship if one of the parties is no longer capable of adapting.

There is a beautiful song written by the late, great jazz pianist Bill Evans titled, "The Two Lonely People." The lyrics, written by Carol Hall, speak of two lonely people who sit "idly staring." She could very well be talking about a flat 3rd or 3rd interval relationship gone bad, murdered by boredom.

The Two Lonely People

The two lonely people sat silently staring
Their eyes looking coldly ahead
The two lonely people once loved and were caring
But now it's all over and dead
They don't know what happened
They can't think what happened
They had something fine on their own
But the two lonely people have turned into statues
Yes turned into statues of stone
The world was their moon once
The yellow ones
It held all their hopes and their dreams
But time came and broke them
Reality woke them
The world's not so pretty as it seems
For all that once mattered
Is old now and battered
But must it be shattered in two
The two lonely people
Would give all their life
Yes give all their life
If they knew... The two lonely people sat silently staring
Their eyes looking coldly ahead

> The two lonely people sat silently staring
> Their eyes looking coldly ahead
> (Evans & Hall, 1971)

The intervals of the flat 3rd and 3rd, with their respective inversions, are some of the most fluid relationships to negotiate. Yet, for some, these pairings are too soft, too saccharine and potentially unchallenging for their tastes. Some like it hot, some not.

Example 8:
Lolo and Stephen — Flat 3rd

Lolo and I form a flat 3rd/6th interval relationship. Without being conscious of our interval influences, we easily draw an accurate portrayal of the flat 3rd/6th. Lolo is an artist who works with acrylics and *repujado*. *Repujado* is a Spanish technique of forming images in thin metal and molding it onto wood, in her case, wooden boxes whereas I devote my interests to music and writing. Both being artists, we share many of the same requirements inherent in our chosen fields: solitude, beauty and a peaceful environment. We also share a love of cooking, Lolo being the master, and me being the devoted sous chef and the official and willing taster.

When there is time for a walk, we both go together. In the afternoons, we go to the beach for our sunset viewing and our Margarita reward. We spend a lot of time together. So much so, that we often need to create individual space. Remember, that this interval has the challenge of being too much the same.

Inversion to the 6ᵗʰ

The flat 3ʳᵈ, as open and playful as it is, can also invert. And, when it does, it creates a romantic and sensitive interval, the 6ᵗʰ, which is capable of showing new maturity and sensitivity. This interval combination just keeps getting better and better with age.

The flat 3ʳᵈ/6ᵗʰ inversion transforms from languid, sweet and melancholic to earthly, joyful and positive. In comparison to the flat 3ʳᵈ, which creates a feeling of mild dissonance and uplift, the 6ᵗʰ conveys a heartfelt expression of peace and floating; it exudes a maturity that the flat 3ʳᵈ is lacking. While the flat 3ʳᵈ is romantic, the 6ᵗʰ is globally inclusive. Romantically speaking, the flat 3ʳᵈ could be considered lustful compared to the wiser, more sensitive 6ᵗʰ. Both intervals are warm, friendly, cooperative and joyful. Yet, with the 6ᵗʰ, there is just more room in which to play, since the distance between the two notes in the 6ᵗʰ are far greater than it is in the flat 3ʳᵈ; with this added space comes a softening and consequently, a more open heart.

Example 9:
Christy and Dave - Flat 3ʳᵈ

Christy and Dave form what I feel is a perfect example of the flat 3ʳᵈ interval relationship in its inverted state, the 6ᵗʰ. For their young age they express a level of maturity, a sensitivity that is not normally found until one's relationship has matured and survived the tests and trials of life. Prior to their first meeting, both were in a passive relationship with someone else. Unfortunately, I don't have data on the intervals they were experiencing at the time but, from the day Christy and Dave met they were unquestionably in love. From that moment, their worlds instantly changed. They knew they were meant for each other.

The ability to move together, laugh and love together and find comfort in the arms of each other, are some of the characteristics of the flat 3rd/6th inversion. Christy and Dave are prime examples of these benefits and attributes. Luckily, they haven't fallen into the trap of sameness. They are wise and sensitive enough to have found jobs and pursuits separate from each other, thus avoiding constantly being together. They make private time for each other and share themselves well with their chosen group of mutual friends.

Unlike with the dissonant intervals where a certain degree of "rub" can be found, they shy away from tension, dominance and conflict. If you were around them, you most likely would see them kissing rather than fighting. When they are in their inverted interval, the 6th, they exhibit a wonderful sense of compassion for others, a respect for the glories of nature and a desire to uplift those around them.

You can see that the flat 3rd interval has both its rewards and its issues. Fortunately, however, the interval relationship can be easily resolved with a bit of BALANCE and sensitivity. The Centering Balance Meditation (found at the end of the book) can help open your heart so that this octave jump (inverting) comes with ease and awareness.

3ʳᵈ Interval

Tonality, that universal Earth out of which diversity can spring

Leonard Bernstein (The Unanswered Questions: Six Talks at Harvard, 1976)

Partner Birth Month		Your Birth Month		Partner Birth Month
		January	➡	May
		February	➡	June
		March	➡	July
		April	➡	August
January	➡	May	➡	September
February	➡	June	➡	October
March	➡	July	➡	November
April	➡	August	➡	December
May	➡	September		
June	➡	October		
July	➡	November		
August	➡	December		

Staff

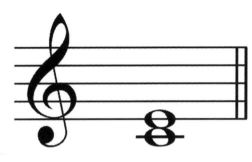

3rd Interval

C-E

Mildly Dissonant

Characteristics

Joyful

Strong

Harmonious

Virtuous

Cheerful

Easy-Going

Quiet

Musical References

First Notes of *While Shepherds Watch Their Flocks by Night* - Kidzone

First Notes of *I Can't Get Started* - George Gershwin as performed by Doug McKenzie

I t's time to grab that imaginary guitar and give the string another twist. Tighten that string up until you reach the next interval, the 3rd. How sweet it sounds, like the music of a Greek fishing village, or the mandolins playing on the waterways of Palermo. Get out your mandolin and play C and E together to hear the sweetness of this interval.

We now come to the most joyous and easy going of all the intervals, that of the 3rd. Thirds are one of the more popular musical intervals found in the study of relationships. If you return to the chapter titled Research, you will see that a large portion of the relationships in my study have this interval. It is the most general of sounds in Western music and is found in pop, country and ethnic songs throughout the Western world. Most people easily relate to the wholesome and positive effect this interval provides. The keywords are joyous, easy going, harmonious, and strong. On the downside, the interval holds, like the flat 3rd, the potential for inertia and boredom. This interval also creates a feeling of hope and sweetness; it is often used in hymns.

People of the 3rd relationship generally get along well and have few challenges. Though not the richest, or deepest of relationships, 3^{rds} are definitely easy going and fun to be around. The level of depth found in the more dissonant intervals is absent here. This interval enjoys lightheartedness and playfulness. When found in the workplace, it means cooperation and dependability. In school or amongst friends it usually leads to long-term relationships and associations. Others view this pairing as dependable, solid and reliable. Few challenges face the 3^{rds}, however, they can become boring through their blind affection for one another; it may be hard to tell one partner from the other.

In counterpoint, the 3^{rds} can move in any direction together but are limited, like the flat 3rd, in the duration of their movement. That is to say, these two notes sound great for a short time together until the mind catches on to the repetition. Then apathy sets in as the movement becomes predictable and routine. The challenge here is definitely individuality and diversification. Survival is dependent on creating a degree, however small, of independence. The force and energy generated by their interwoven closeness can be off-putting to others, often creating a barrier excluding everyone around them. When encountered between an employer and an employee, others in the workplace may feel left on the outside of a perceived private conversation. In a relationship, boredom, due to routine, can easily set in. This can cause one partner to stray, looking for more excitement. There is a definite need to mix it up and keep it fresh. In all aspects of their lives, spice is nice!

If you find yourself in this interval connection and it's not working, look for ways you may be adding to the sameness. Shake yourself awake and approach the situation from a different angle. Don't blame the other party when you can make the difference. In this interval, the people involved want to be together. When you make the proper correction, the relationship will automatically flow again as it did when you excitedly and enthusiastically got together for the first time. Remember, as a couple, not to put everyone to sleep with your predictability. Show your individual flare every chance you get.

When not stuck in a routine, the 3rd interval brings joy and lightheartedness to those around them. They are great entertainers and impeccable hosts. Be thankful if you're in a relationship of this nature: great times, friendships and romance are part of the package if you stay aware of your potential challenges.

Interestingly, in music, the flat 3rd and the 3rd, and their inversions, are the only intervals out of the 12 that indicate they belong to a definite key. None of the other intervals shows any tendency to have a defined home base. The second note in the pairing of both the flat 3rd and 3rd tells us to which home key it belongs. For the flat

3rd, the key is found a minor 3rd higher. For example, C and E flat, forming the flat 3rd, belong to the key of E flat. While C and E, forming the 3rd, belong to the key of C.

What this means for our interval relationships is that these two groupings have a home base. Both are very auspicious for family connections. Unlike the other nine options, the flat 3rd and 3rd don't float uncommitted through life. They are dedicated and family oriented intervals, complete with home roots. So, if you are in one of these relationships, you are in a unique and excellent situation when compared to the more challenging dissonant intervals.

This interval, along with the flat 3rd, is the only two intervals that can express joy and sadness, elation and introspection. While the other intervals can show power, independence and emotional fire, the 3rds express love and connectedness. If this is your interval relationship, be thankful for the opportunity to develop this love and connection.

I knew another couple in Southern California who were in a relationship of a 3rd. I had known them for better than 30 years; they were my neighbors in our quiet little beachside village. The reason I mention them here is that these two people were classic 3^{rds}. Every day that they walked past my house they were holding hands. He always wore the same outfit: brown Madras checkered short-sleeved shirt, khaki shorts and running shoes. What made them stand out as 3^{rds}, besides their continued togetherness, was that she also wore the exact matching outfit. There was not a day gone by that they wore something different from each other. I never saw them walking with anyone else, nor did they seem to invite friends to their home. They were complete in and of themselves, a sort of Bobsey Twin singular phenomenon and an extreme example of "sameness" that can be found in the 3rd.

Inversion to the Flat 6th

The inversion of this interval forms a softer and more open formatted interval called the flat 6th. By gaining an appreciation of the connectedness of these two intervals and how they interact with each other, you will become prepared to invert when you sense that you're in a tight space or a compromised position and could use some resolution. By having notes that are farther apart, the interval-relationship of the 6th has the ability to more gracefully handle the challenges that occur during the day. The added space makes for a comfortable playing field and gives the relationship a more mature version of the 3rd. Remember, you can access the flat 6th anytime while in the 3rd relationship by merely allowing the person, born in the later month of the year, to hold the dominating energy for a while—invert*!*

The flat 6th is an enjoyable image of the 3rd reflected in the mirror and takes you to a more mature vista. While your 3rd relationship was ever so intertwined—romantically, emotionally, socially and familially—the 6th opens up and releases those binds formed by that tightness. Here is where you can really relax in the relationship. The interval of the 3rd shows the capacity of giving and love whereas the flat 6th inversion embraces those around them with that love.

4th Interval

The piano ain't got no wrong notes

Thelonious Monk

Partner Birth Month		Your Birth Month		Partner Birth Month
		January	➡	June
		February	➡	July
		March	➡	August
		April	➡	September
		May	➡	October
January	➡	June	➡	November
February	➡	July	➡	December
March	➡	August		
April	➡	September		
May	➡	October		
June	➡	November		
July	➡	December		

Staff

4th Interval

C-F

Consonant

Characteristics

Serene

Weightless

Non-Commital

Individualistic

Easy-Going

Distant

Agreeable

Musical References

Oh, Christmas Tree

Here Comes the Bride - Richard Wagner

Album *"My Favorite Things"* - John Coltrane with McCoy Tyner on piano

Freedom Jazz Dance - Eddie Harris, Performed by Brian Auger & Rudy Rotta Band

A gain, you are going to tune the string on your imaginary guitar higher until you hear the next interval. It's called the 4th. Try playing C and F to hear how this sounds.

4ths are the first interval in the harmonic progression that has the ability to float. Whereas 3rd long for togetherness and companionship, 4ths can remain slightly disconnected to each other without jeopardizing their relationship. The relationship between the two notes is now of far enough distance as to not create an immediate longing for each other. Their gravitational pull has been neutralized. With this comes a feeling of floating openness and lightness. Here is where you will find, for the first time, a relationship that is apparently not in need of each other's energy, yet consonantly and often joyously united. When you encounter this interval in music, unlike the flat 3rd and 3rd, you detect no compelling *desire* to co join, no *desire* to resolve. These two notes are individually quite happy just being. That is not to say that they are not in a relationship. In fact, they love being together, they just don't need to show it. This interval creates a feeling of serenity, weightlessness, and individuality. This interval can be heard in popular music such as "Oh, Christmas Tree" and "Here Comes the Bride"

Being around people in the relationship of a 4th can be very frustrating at times. It often feels as though they each regularly go off and do their own thing. The fact is they do exactly that. To succeed in this relationship both parties must understand that cooperation will often not appear too co-operative, group efforts often seem individualistic and unconnected, and one or the other may appear to be uncaring. The key here is to know that it is only "all appearances". This truly may be a case of what you see is not what you get. 4ths are a pure consonance, a mathematically close connection. These same characteristics appear similar to those found with the interval of the 2nd, however, the difference is that with the 4th, there is much more freedom and relaxation than found in the 2nd. Also, the 2nd expresses a tendency to create dissonance and friction more easily than the 4th.

The interval of the 4th was used extensively in jazz from the 1960s to the present and was ushered into mainstream music by pianists like McCoy Tyner. Tyner used 4ths in his left hand to create washes of sound behind the saxophone of John Coltrane, setting up floating and often strong textures from which Coltrane could launch his musical flights of fancy. One notable recording Tyner made was with Coltrane playing "My Favorite Things," written by Richard Rogers. In this piece you can hear Tyner's left hand playing an unremitting series of chords based on 4ths. The classic jazz composition "Freedom Jazz Dance" by Eddie Harris based its entire melodic structure on 2nds and 4ths.

Pop artists like Sting have incorporated 4ths into compositions to help neutralize the incessant pop sound of sonorous 3rds and 6ths. Remember, 3rds can get boring very quickly. Listen to the very first chord of Sting's "Fields of Gold" to get a feel for the hollow vastness that 4ths produce.

A featured characteristic of the 4th interval relationship is the observable singularity of each partner. Couples in this relationship often lead separate lives, only coming together on occasion and at the proper time. Since they both silently crave this freedom, the interval of a 4th is ideal for them. If not properly understood, this relationship could be difficult to maintain. Between a parent and child, over-control of the child will only cause more separation. For 4th, freedom is essential for both parties, at any age.

Between lovers, don't expect the closeness seen in 3rds and unisons. You may be best served by accepting the spiritual space inherent between you. *Not* being attached at the hip will be your strongest form of connection. 4ths are similar to 2nds in that both intervals together experience what seems like unconnected lives. The

2nds find a degree of difficulty and challenge in this distance while the 4th manages to revel in their separation. 4ths can be like two people going in two directions at the same time yet always showing up sooner or later again as a functioning couple.

One 4th couple I know live a unique life together. I rarely see them with each other and when I do, they still don't seem together. During the day, they both go off and do their own thing, but at night when there is a social gathering, they arrive together, talk and mingle separately with their respective friends, and then rejoin as a couple to return home. Their marriage is seemingly sound and the love between them obvious. They are just 4ths, floating, non-committal, light and open.

Here, the word "openness" refers to the "floating" mentioned earlier. But again, unlike the 2nd, it's not a "distance from" type of openness, but a freedom to be "apart from." That freedom is with agreement and consent from both people in the relationship. Also, unlike the 2nd, there is a sense of calm and lightness in the separation of the energies rather than a sense of conflict. The 4th is one of the only three "consonant" intervals, along with the 5th and the unison/octave. Even though you can successfully float in this interval, you make up one of the most pure, strong and grounded structures in the musical world.

Example 10:
Betty and David - 4th

Betty and David formed a perfect example of the 4th interval relationship. Their attraction to each other was strong and vibrant. They allowed space to happen between each other. And, they conducted their lives with moderate independence and self-direction. Viewed from the outside, their relationship appeared to float; they were definitely not joined at the hip. As a couple, they formed an independent, yet cohesive bond.

They lived such a freeform 4th interval that they found comfort and connection even while maintaining separate homes. Their work, individually, took them to opposite sides of the province often not seeing each other for days. Yet, somehow, it seemed a perfect fit. They both loved and honored the freedom that the 4th interval allowed. How the relationship would have fared if someday children were included remains to be seen.

This interval-relationship seemed best meant for solid individuals who possessed confidence and maturity and the ability to live at a distance from their partner. For David and Betty, the option of having been in a close 3rd or flat 3rd interval-relationship may have proven to be too suffocating—too tightly bound. Their individual lifestyles dictated that they maintain their independence to the fullest, while also having the comforts of rich social interactions together. The interval of the 4th was, for them, a perfect fit.

When presented with a lifestyle such as theirs, where physical distance over lengthy periods of time was a norm, the 4th and 5th intervals are often the best choice. The unison relationship tends to disintegrate with separation, while the flat 2nd and 2nd are energetically too unstable to easily survive for long. Two people in the relationship of a flat 3rd and 3rd would, by the nature of the interval, just not accept being apart for extended periods of time. Again, we come back to how each interval has its unique offering, providing a relationship option that is best suited for the prevailing circumstances and conditions. Be sensitive to your interval relationship and determine if it's the most suited for you inner needs.

Inversion to the 5th

The interval of a 4th changes into a 5th when the bottom note moves up one octave, inverting. This is achieved by conscious and deliberate physical relaxation, followed by a soothing surrendering into your higher self. When that happens, the vagueness and floating feeling that 4ths project change into the more firm and reliable 5th. This is moving into the heart space, out of the head, and allows you to "sing differently." You can move the relationship forward in terms of decision making, texture and intensity and to a more gracious and balanced plane. Here, in the 5th, is where more *room* for resolution can be found. Since both parties in the relationship of the 4th are somewhat non-committal, 4ths often need to transform to the 5th to bring about important changes and make concrete decisions.

When you find yourselves, as 4ths, in a challenging situation or are feeling unfulfilled by the relationship, when you feel as though you want to be closer than the interval will allow and the walls between you and your lover are in the way, check to see which one of you is more headstrong. If it's the person with the first chronological birth month, try relaxing a bit and let your partner dominate for a moment. You may find that everything opens up to greater possibilities of resolution or success. Become the interval of the 5th and be stable for a while. Allow your being to be bathed by the newness and grace of your inversion and after you have absorbed the benefits of that experience, return back to your partner and resume, carrying this new lightness and certainty into your interactions and inner dynamics. When you get through the tough times, return once again to the interval of the 4th with your new found strength and firmness.

Flat 5th Interval

Harmony requires us to change along with the whole. If you open your-self to the hum of the world—if you live in the present rather than in your idea of it—it will change you

Phillip Shepherd (Out of Our Heads, 2013)

Partner Birth Month		Your Birth Month		Partner Birth Month
		January	➡	July
		February	➡	August
		March	➡	September
		April	➡	October
		May	➡	November
		June	➡	December
January	➡	July		
February	➡	August		
March	➡	September		
April	➡	October		
May	➡	November		
June	➡	December		

Staff

Flat 5th Interval

C-F#/Gb

Absolute Dissonance

Characteristics

Hostile

Mysterious

Destructive

Adversarial

Explosive

Imbalance

Powerful

Musical References

Purple Haze - The Jimi Henrix Experience

Maria - Leonard Bernstein, West Side Story

The Simpsons Theme Song - Danny Elfman

Up to this point the flowing growth process for each interval has been toward expansion, from unison to the 4th. However, with the flat 5th, the peak of individuation has met its apex and will begin the slow decent back to unity, the octave. The flat 5th holds the unique position of being the division point in this spiritual process.

Go ahead and tighten that one string up a little more and produce this next interesting interval. Alternately, you can play C and Gb on your guitar or piano.

The flat 5th is also called the augmented 4th. This little number is without a doubt the most intriguing of all the intervals. It is described as hostile, adverse, destructive and mysterious. It sits halfway between the unison and the octave and creates the dividing point where, the flat 2nd, 2nd, flat 3rd, 3rd and 4th begin to mirror themselves as the 5th, flat 6th, 6th, flat 7th and 7th. Even though it's situated between two of the most consonant interval, the 4th and 5th, the flat 5th is the most dissonant interval.

You can see the connection made between December and June in the image below, an interval relationship of a flat 5th. If you connect any opposing months: January-July; September-March; November-May, etc., you form a flat 5th relationship.

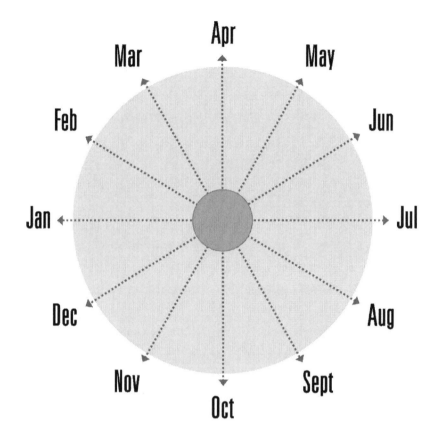

As you can see, the flat 5ᵗʰ divides the circle directly into two equal halves. You could compare the image to the full moon—fully light on one side and totally dark on the other. The characteristic for the flat 5 interval is also like the moon, the combination of two supremely opposing energies. The drawing factor between two people of this interval seems to be that inherent powerful yin/yang attribute. Without exception, every couple I researched who were in the flat 5ᵗʰ relationship showed the same tendencies, they were all unequivocally dependent upon a firm dominant/subdominant matrix.

More often than not, in the flat 5ᵗʰ relationship, the person with more female energy was the dominant party. I can find no obvious explanation for that other than the indications from the data collected. The subdominant member was usually and noticeably docile and regressive in the mix. There is some evidence to suggest that there may have been a flat 5ᵗʰ relationship with one or both of their parents. We have often heard that we marry our father or mother when we choose a mate. One thing is for sure, those who find themselves in the flat 5ᵗʰ relationship *can* be happy and well-adjusted to this particular and strange combination as long as their roles are maintained. While it's not for everyone, it can work. Difficulty arises when the passive member begins to assert him or herself, sparks fly and in a big way! The dominant member can, and most often will, be overly aggressive until the second party resumes their submissive role. There is no room for darkness on the sunny side of the moon.

That goes both ways. The submissive party often likes being in their role. It saves them the hassle of assuming the details of making decisions or holding a commanding lead, something they would usually prefer to avoid.

The flat 5ᵗʰ creates a feeling of suspense, the occult, outer space, and strangeness. This interval was called "The Devil in Music" in the Middle Ages and was banned by the Church due to its nebulous characteristic. The tritone, or 'Devil's Chord' as it was also called, had a long musical history of links to diabolism, from the wholesale banning of it in the Middle Ages, through the Romantic era, then into blues and jazz, and finally, to modern horror film music and death metal. Listen to Jimi Hendrix's "Purple Haze," Leonard Bernstein's "Maria" and the theme from "The Simpsons," written by Danny Elfman, to hear this interval in action. If you are in a relationship with someone and your birth months form a flat 5ᵗʰ, you can gain great understanding of your relationship by going back

1,100 years in history to a time when composers purportedly could face death for using that interval.

Musically, the two notes of the flat 5th are worlds apart in their formation. Taking the root C and its flat 5th (G flat) together and looking at the scale derived from each, neither of these notes is part of the other's home key. Like the two sides of the moon, it's either all light or all dark, there are no shades of grey.

To function in this relationship successfully, it's of absolute importance to understand that both parties cannot be equal. As with the full moon, only one side can be fully seen at any time. If you do require equality, moving apart and seeking someone who will be a flat 2nd, a close facsimile to the flat 5th, may serve you best. Here, you will find more manageability. Remember, this is not an easy combination, it's not for everyone. However, when successfully negotiated, this relationship can be strong and loving, but it takes practice, patience and knowledge.

Example 11:
Francisco and Alice - Flat 5th

I knew a marvelous young man Francisco: gentle, always smiling, loved by everyone. Though he is accomplished at his vocation and well liked socially, he is not one to be noticed or take charge. He prefers to work quietly behind the curtain and let others take the credit and receive the applause. He works honestly and efficiently and often finds his talents in demand but needs the close contact of an authoritative boss (or wife) to stay directed. He married a woman named Alice. Alice is the opposite of Francisco: strong headed, self-directed and always in control. Their relationship functioned very well for being a flat 5th. Her forcefulness and his passivity combined to form a synergetic partnership that serves them both well.

While Francisco and Alice had worked out their flat 5th balance and had achieved a relationship, Alice once showed me an interesting contrast. When another person who was also a flat 5th to her, but in the stronger, more dominant role confronted Alice, the fur began to fly. As they say in the old Western movies, "This town ain't big enough for the both of us!" A head-on collision occurred, and everyone in close proximity left the area until the dust settled. The flat 5th interval often can be explosive, not caring to mask their eruptions from the outside world. When the time comes for exerting dominance, it can happen anywhere, regardless of the social environment they find themselves in. I often see it as a volcano erupting—it's going to happen when and where it finds its outlet. Often, the person holding the dominant position exhibits the social characteristics of forcefulness and control. In order to maintain their sense of balance they seek out a passive partner. The reverse can be said of the passive partner. The power contained in the flat 5th is of the most potent and visceral kinds, potentially explosive, and great restraint must be applied to defuse these inherent social shipwrecks. If you find yourself in an unbalanced flat 5th relationship be prepared to dance, not like a ballet diva but like Muhammad Ali.

I know of another couple in this relationship that came to me after I had posted a chapter on the flat 5th on a social media web page. They too maintained a perfect dominant/subdominant balance, with the woman strongly in the control seat. I saw them at the market one day when she pulled me aside and said that she had read the article and highly disagreed with my synopsis. Her marriage of over 25 years was one of equality and compromise, she insisted. She then turned to her husband, standing very quietly and passively behind her, and commanded: "Tell him! Tell him that what I just said was true!" I almost couldn't refrain from chuckling, as the flat 5th played out predictably before my eyes.

Below is a chart of Lolo and me with two friends, Jay and Carl. Most of the time, between the four of us, our mutual relationship was good, but sometimes challenges would arise between us. *Harmonology* helped me decipher the hidden reasons for those challenges. While two out of three of the relationship connections are flat 3rds and a unison, Jay and I form the flat 5th.

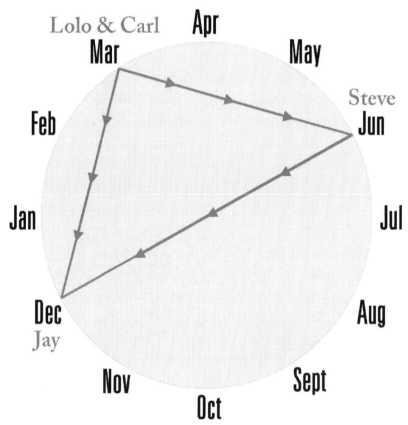

Most of the time, especially when only Carl was present, our social interactions went graciously and smoothly. However, when Jay was present, difficult issues arose that left me at a loss to explain. At times, I felt there was a barrier that was erected between them and us, or more precisely, between Jay and me. It wasn't until I charted out our dynamics that I began to understand the inherent rub that needed a very special attention.

If you look at the chart, you will see that Lolo and Carl are in a unison relationship, as long as they moved in the same direction in their thoughts and actions, there was harmony. I share a flat 3rd relationship with both Lolo and Carl, and they both share a 6th relationship with Jay, which generally has little in the way of issues and challenges. However, the hidden "thorn under the saddle" came by way of the flat 5th between Jay and I. By interjecting the flat 5th into this semi-harmonious grouping, the collective relationship suffered an unbearable level of dissonance and friction. For a while, when Jay was absent, the remaining three of us enjoyed an understandably harmonious and somewhat unchallenged social interaction. But, once the flat 5th was introduced the balance of energies was compromised. At the time, had I known how to recognize the challenges of this interval, I would have had the tools to reduce the tension by reducing the resistance. By doing so, I could have created more space between Jay and I that would have allowed for healing. Many of you intuitively do that already. But, having the knowledge of *Harmonology* can give you the upper hand in resolving conflicts found in your relationships.

It's a good practice to make similar charts for your family or friends. By doing so, a world of unseen knowledge will open to you, offering you a greater understanding of the dynamics at play. You will read much more about making these charts in the chapter titled *Charting Family Dynamics*.

Example 12:
Steve and Jay - Flat 5th

I met Jay at a fundraiser in Mexico, where I live. She was a very pretty, thin and well-dressed young lady with a great voice and a seductive presentation. One could say that she fell upon the eyes like vanilla ice cream in the heat of the desert. We were to perform together for an upcoming music event that showcased some highly talented local unknowns along with a few amateurish wannabes. Upon meeting Jay, I felt a certain distance between us that I haven't normally encountered with other professional vocalists. I thought it might just be due to the newness of the relationship. Perhaps over time the distance would shorten, like the tide slowly coming in, and we could collaborate on something of musical value. In the past, most singers quickly recognized the musical support and empathy I offered, but not this time.

That evening, Jay and I performed at a respectful artistic level and the audience was duly impressed. However, the gap in our mutual energy flow was obvious to me. It was as though I was trying to get good gas mileage while driving into a strong headwind, and with the brake on! When I first met Jay she introduced me to her husband, a burly Mexican man named Carl, who was descended from Anglo and Mexican heritage, a definite advantage for functioning in the business world of this country. They were as the equal mix of coffee and milk in a great *café con leche*. Carl was a building contractor, very adept and well nuanced at his craft and an immediately likable guy. Lolo got along well with Jay and

Carl. There was a 'birds of a feather' *simpatico* flowing between them. As for me, Carl was like a long lost brother. We could look at one another with a recognition that seemed to be beyond the present time.

As I progressed in working with Jay, I became frustrated by our inability to communicate with and trust each other, two very important ingredients necessary to perform music at a higher artistic level. Every time we would rehearse I would be left with the feeling that nothing of depth was accomplished. It was as though we were driving in the same car but with two steering wheels, going two separate directions. After a time, for me this led to much frustration.

It wasn't until I developed *Harmonology* that I recognized from where these issues arose. Jay being B, and me being F, we slice the circle right down the middle by our flat 5th relationship—the Devil's Interval! The flat 5th interval is composed of two notes that have no musical relationship to each other; they are from two separate keys and as far apart musically as two notes can get. Remember the phrase: "This town ain't big enough for the both of us." In the middle of this group of friends now lies the threat of a power play between Jay and me, and is where all the smooth interactions that came before have the possibility of falling apart. Both Jay and I individually are strong and valid, but when combined, prove to be too bold to hold harmony for very long. To be successful in the flat 5th interval-relationship, one of the partners holds the dominance while one stays submissive. For now, with my knowledge of the flat 5th, I can handle the thorny issues that most likely will arise in the future between the four of us, thanks to *Harmonology*.

Summing up the flat 5th relationship: it is strong, unbalanced and volatile. Only those who can handle the heat need get in the frying pan. Be assured however, those who can consciously deal with this level of challenge make great partners, good neighbors and strong parents. Often, just by being aware of the flat 5th challenge, the potential damage done could be somewhat neutralized. Caution must be used, though. If neutralized too much, the relationship weakens its bonds and faces the potential for disintegration. This interval thrives on the dominant/subdominant interplay. In a sense, though I have emphasized balance throughout this book, balance here means something different. Only those in the flat 5th relationship can be the final judges of balance.

Lateralization

This interval offers a wonderful and unique opportunity to relocate one's center of consciousness. In the Western World the center of our consciousness is often dominated by the left-brain. A person who is "left-brained" is often said to be more logical, analytical, and objective, while a person who is "right-brained" is said to be more intuitive, thoughtful, and subjective.

While this theory of "lateralization," first pioneered by Roger W. Sperry and awarded the Nobel Prize in 1981, is now considered outdated, it leads us to the concept of spiritual gender identification. Each of us is comprised of both male and female potentials and traits. The brain is no exception. The spiritually masculine left-brain is often described as being better at: language, logic, critical thinking, numbers and reasoning.

Spiritually, the right side of the brain is considered feminine and best at expressive and creative tasks. Some of the abilities that are popularly associated with the right side of the brain include: recognizing faces, expressing emotions, music, reading emotions, color, images, intuition, and creativity.

Again, with lateralization, we see the two sides of the moon in play—masculine and feminine. The left-brain thinking of the past generations has produced great innovations and inventions, from the airplane to the Internet. But, it has also spawned horrendous wars and hideous devices of mass annihilation. The male dominated thinking brought about the Inquisition, complete with ingenious and demonic methods of torture that are still in use today by governments, the military and drug cartels. It's well past time to move to a matriarchal world and towards creativity, love and compassion for all.

The relationship interval of the flat 5th offers the precious chance to go from head to heart, aggression to compassion. As I mentioned above, when the subdominant partner in this interval attempts to gain equilibrium, chaos is sure to ensue, as the dominant partner will work to regain supreme control. Rather than continuing to butt heads, a move to a different way of thinking presents itself.

In my first book *Counterpoint to Reality*, I shared some of my experiences and healing modalities learned through Ayahuasca, the visionary plant extract from the Amazon. During one of my sessions I was taught that by shifting my thinking from the head to the heart space one would receive protection, inspiration and connection. That wisdom provided its proof when I was confronted by my own internal dilemma. I found the shift to be profound and dramatic.

In the flat 5th interval, and in all the intervals, shifting from the headspace to the heart space automatically diffuses the potential chaos, and eliminates the confrontational aspects of the opposing energies. A profound healing then occurs and the potential for deeper levels of loving become available.

Flat 5th Interval

I know of two married friends in this interval that, one of them, during the primary stages of their relationship, was very ac-quiescent to the more dominant other. At the time, it worked very well. Over the past several years, the subdominant partner has started to regret his lesser position and has attempted to assert some control over his participation in the partnership. As usual, it resulted in quite a bit of friction and confrontation. Then, as he moved into his heart space through meditation and awareness, the flame of ag-gression found less and less fuel from which to feed, and now their relationship is experiencing a beautiful and passionate reconnection.

By allowing this change to have taken place, no one was hurt nor did the marriage suffer. To the contrary, a new of level sensitivity was attained that was considered by both to be life-transformative.

So that you can feel this movement from the head to the heart, I am including a short relaxation meditation. When you per-form this exercise, consciously feel the softening of your being. See if you can sense the shift of energy, a movement from restraint to openness. Please go to Heart Meditation to access this exercise. Done frequently, this practice will establish peace within you and make you feel more independent, and love will be more of a giving; you'll have so much peace you'll want to share it. You will be return-ing to a source in yourself that is always there.

5th Interval

Life is not always a matter of holding good cards, but sometimes, playing a poor hand well

Jack London

Partner Birth Month		Your Birth Month		Partner Birth Month
		January	➡	August
		February	➡	September
		March	➡	October
		April	➡	November
		May	➡	December
		June		
		July		
January	➡	August		
February	➡	September		
March	➡	October		
April	➡	November		
May	➡	December		

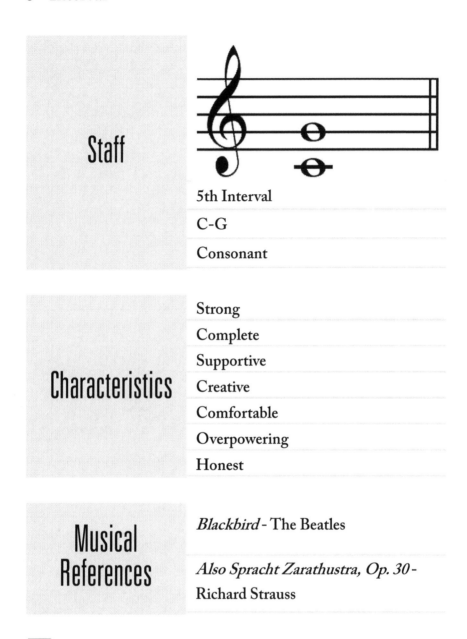

Staff	
	5th Interval
	C-G
	Consonant

Characteristics	
	Strong
	Complete
	Supportive
	Creative
	Comfortable
	Overpowering
	Honest

Musical References	
	Blackbird - The Beatles
	Also Spracht Zarathustra, Op. 30 - Richard Strauss

In music, 5^{ths} are the fundamental structures that support many of the creative melodies that move around them. Often, the 5^{ths} create the primal and neutral support needed to fulfill the structural needs, while the unison melodies define the "color" tones, those that describe sadness or joy. 5^{ths} are the pillars of the musical social community; they form a solid and strong foundation that gives those dependent upon them the security to venture forth into more refined realms of harmony.

Two people in this interval exhibit the feeling of power, firmness, strength, family, responsibility, courage and truth. The combination is mathematically simple—a ratio of 1:2 or the upper note is one half the value of the root tone. In 5^{ths}, the bottom note is considered the root and the dominant of the two. Therefore, the person born in the first of the two months holds the final decision power, though that does not mean holding authority over the other person. More precisely, both people have autonomy. However, the primary and fundamental person needs to be given the position of caretaker, the one who either initiates or decides upon an issue in cooperation with the other.

In traditional counterpoint, 5^{ths} are forbidden to move in a parallel manner; they cannot progress in identical directions. Yet, over the years, this musical rule has softened to allow the movement of parallel 5^{ths} for the unique sonic effect they produce. It was said that parallel 5^{ths} created a hollow and weak sound that violated their inherent strength. But, just listen to any hard rock or grunge band to correct that view! Played as these musicians do, parallel 5^{ths} are the essence of power. After all, they are not called power chords without a reason! For our relationships, this means not using your combined power for extended periods of time or for gaining the upper hand. Always be sensitive to the conditions around you.

The success of this interval relationship comes in the ability for both parties to be independent while also being dependent. In other words, this comes about when one of the two people involved is allowed to pursue different interests and is able to venture alone from the relationship. For example, the relationship grows stronger and more successful if one or both parties have separate jobs, interests, friends and hobbies, but can come home to share with the other in a loving and fulfilled way.

The danger inherent in the 5^{ths} relationship is when both sides do everything together. As in music, it potentially creates a hollow sound and can be too strong for anyone else to tolerate for very long. 5^{ths} are powerful! I have known couples that dominate and usurp the focus of attention in social gatherings to such an extent that those around them feel uncomfortable.

Going back to the chapter on 4^{ths}, you learned that they, like their inversion, 5^{ths}, create a space where the relationship can rest and enjoy life at a slower pace. Unlike the dissonant flat 2nd and 2nd, flat 7th and 7th, the desire to achieve "individual greatness" is diminished. Interval relationships of 5^{ths} have already done this in past lives and now look to be stable, connected and strong.

5^{ths} are unquestionably the most solid of all the intervals, the relationship "Rock of Gibraltar." In music, they are the power chords played by every amateur guitarist in his or her garage. 5^{ths} are the foundational structure in the brass of the classical orchestra. Key words here are: stable, strong, overpowering, supportive, regimented, completeness, comfort and creativity. Where flat 5^{ths} hold potential for chaos and instability, 5^{ths} contain the promise of foundation and calm. After the unison (1:1) and the octave (2:1), 5^{ths} (3:2) are the most simple of integer ratios (mathematical ratio of the frequencies). Two tones are consonant if their frequencies are related by a small integer ratio. This means they are fundamentally harmonious and stable, and that's a great thing when it comes to relationships. This interval creates a feeling of completeness, comfort, and creativity.

To hear the 5th, go to the guitar strings and tighten one higher to the interval of the fifth or go to the piano and play C and

G together. The birth months of March and October, as an example, form a 5th. This combination should get along very co-operatively and smoothly. Any 5th relationship holds the promise of being firm and reliable, not only to themselves but to everyone around them. They become the trusted workhorses at the office or the reliable and supportive friends you have associated with. By listening to the introduction notes of "Blackbird" by the Beatles, or the incredibly strong opening notes of Richard Strauss' "Also Spracht Zarathustra," one can easily sense the amazing power of this interval; it's clean, unadorned and pristine in its sound.

As reliable and dependable as this relationship may be, it can also produce more brute power than can be successfully maintained. Think again of that kid in the garage with his guitar on overkill! 5^{ths} can be the bull in the china shop. The challenge is to keep it easy and simple, don't try to be everything to everyone. Those in this relationship need to know that they don't know it all and, above all, they must make room for others—be sensitive.

When faced with a challenging 5th as a boss, child or lover, be attentive to the constant possibility of butting heads. Open your third eye to see what is really happening and again, be graceful like a matador—allow that bull to charge past your imaginary cape without bodily contact. However, remember that you may also be the power problem here. As a couple, the 5th can be offsetting to others. They can often become a private party to the exclusion of those who travel in their orbit; their strength and insularity can make it very uncomfortable for others to be around.

Example 13:
Ted and Karla - 5ᵗʰ

Ted and Karla are a couple I have known for many years. I worked with Ted and, at times, we encountered challenges. Overall, our professional relationship was good, though often difficult. It was when he married Karla that I saw the unbridled power of 5ᵗʰˢ. Karla was born in March, Ted in October—they are a 5ᵗʰ apart. The marriage was a strong and loving affair. However, at one point the two of them decided to pair up in business. One was very creative, and the other had a great sense of the business side of their life.

I remember one day while in a business meeting with them, an issue came up regarding the abilities of a third party. Up until this point the person in question was doing an exemplary job and receiving much praise and kudos from Ted and Karla. Suddenly, for some unexpected reason, they decided that this person was no longer performing well and was of little value to them. The sheer power of the 5ᵗʰˢ took over and created a day filled with chaos and tears. It soon became my job to dismiss the offending person as soon as possible. I felt as though an armored tank had just driven through the middle of my day, crushing everyone in its path.

While the power of the 5ᵗʰˢ was in full bloom, there was nothing to ameliorate the devastation happening in that room. Everyone in earshot was diving for cover, and anger and frustration permeated the building. It wasn't until I discovered this system, *Harmonology*, that I understood the dynamics of that day; it was just one of the potentials that was available when interacting with a 5th interval.

Had I known this then, I would have asked the couple to shift the power from Karla to Ted. Remember, Karla was born in March and Ted in October. And that, as you recall, forms a 5th, (D and A). But if Karla had given up a bit of her dominance and allowed Ted to hold the foundation, their relationship would convert to 4^{ths} (A and D), a much softer and non-committal and floating manner. In this case, March and October, when reversed are October and March, they become 4^{ths}. If they or I knew this in advance, the situation could have been prevented; no one would have lost face and the project would have been settled in a fair and friendly manner to the benefit of all.

Inversion to the 4th

Now comes the moment when you ask why you need to invert to the 4th and what are the benefits? The inversion is not only valuable and necessary, but in fact, you do it constantly and intuitively every day.

Picture in your mind two columns standing strong and tall, almost immovable. That is you and your partner while in the relationship of a 5th. You are the pillars of the community, reliable and dependable. It can become tiring always being the mainstay to your other collective relationships. The requirement that you place upon your partner to sustain this strength can start to become suffocating and the expectations of constant reliability can be too demanding to maintain. This is where the inversion to the 4th becomes pivotal.

5th Interval

The interval of the 4th produces a more vague, non-committal and floating quality that blends well in social and business situations. You will feel less commitment to regimentation, and more individual strength and flexibility to exert your personal charm and influence. Though there is more room in the 5th for psychic expansion, there is less daunting responsibility in the 4th. After inverting to the 4th relationship, you will find you can play a bit more on the edge and can express a certain degree of flair. You will still be strong, but now expressing that serenity, lightness and openness inherent in the inversion to the 4th.

Again, using the provided meditations can greatly assist in this transformation so that more of our relationships can be healed.

Flat 6th Interval

If music is the food of love, play on

William Shakespeare (Twelfth Night, 1:1)

Partner Birth Month		Your Birth Month		Partner Birth Month
		January	➡	September
		February	➡	October
		March	➡	November
		April	➡	December
		May		
		June		
		July		
		August		
January	➡	September		
February	➡	October		
March	➡	November		
April	➡	December		

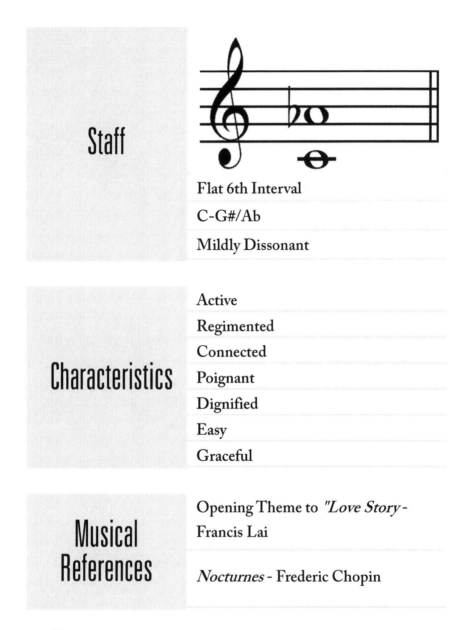

Staff

Flat 6th Interval

C-G#/Ab

Mildly Dissonant

Characteristics

Active

Regimented

Connected

Poignant

Dignified

Easy

Graceful

Musical References

Opening Theme to *"Love Story* - Francis Lai

Nocturnes - Frederic Chopin

Again, let's tune that string on the imaginary two-stringed guitar to an even higher note and bring it to the interval of a flat 6th. This interval can be found on the piano or guitar by playing C and Ab. The sound is sweet and melodic; the interval is rich and melancholic. Though considered mildly dissonant, the flat 6th feels like home. People in this interval-relationship have a *simpatico* feeling for each other, a close hidden bond that forms the foundation of their relationship. This is one of the intervals of love.

Flat 6ths, like their sister the 3rd, enjoy a high degree of harmony and ease; they show dignity but lightness. This interval-relationship melds into each other with grace and smoothness. However, dissimilarly, the flat 6th is somewhat more reserved in its display of romantic emotion, though there is plenty of that behind the curtain. This musical interval creates a feeling of poignancy as is evidenced in the opening theme music for the movie "Love Story", and also found in many of Chopin's Nocturnes.

Issues connected with this interval are similar to those of the 3rd, namely boredom and sameness. Care must be taken not to allow routine to dominate and cause a loss of individuality. At times, with the attraction being so compelling, this interval-relationship can forget that there are two separate individuals involved. When this happens, balance needs to be restored. Consider separating for a while and doing something on your own, there are plenty of opportunities to get back together and move in that parallel fashion once again. According to counterpoint, two notes that make a flat 6th have 3 options: both can go forward together, one can go forward while the other rests, or they can go in separate directions altogether.

The human mind has the ability to detect patterns easily, and when 3rds with flat 6ths, and flat 3rds with 6ths move together for too long the mind knows what is coming next. The immediate result is boredom for the listener. Have you ever noticed that when you hear a pop tune on the radio you are able to sing along before the tune has even had the chance to finish? That sometimes is a case of too much predictability. It may be fun for a short while but it leads to the doldrums if sustained for too long. Don't find yourself in that position with your relationships lest you start seeing a lot of yawning by your surrounding company. Be light, be playful and most of all, be unpredictable.

Example 14:
Mike and Monick - Flat 6th

Mike and Monick have been married for over 40 years and form the "picture perfect" interval of a flat 6th. With their relationship, you can get a glimpse into the dynamic of this combination. Monick was born in January and Mike in September. Most times that I have visited them I found them at the kitchen table, just the two of them, having a cigarette and a cup of coffee. They exuded an air of permanence, relaxation and peacefulness. They have lived in the same house for most of their married lives, and Mike even had his workshop located on the property so as not to be too far from Monick. While Mike took care of the outside chores and worked in his shop to provide for their income, Monick formed the foundation and center point of the home. They, visually, fit together without conflict or tension and gave off the impression of being one complete harmonious unit. Their love for each other was easy to see, their being in agreement was obvious and their interwoven and fluid movement expressed what the 3rd is all about: togetherness, harmony and syncopation. Musically speaking, they were "in the groove." 3rds, when functioning harmoniously, are a joy to be around. Both Mike and Monick expressed a great infectious sense of calm. With that composure came the ability for each to invert at will, and often, thus creating the space necessary so as not to become stale and robotic. With Mike and Monick, the success in their relationship came from the peace in their hearts and their ability to give and take with sensitivity and intuition. Again, inverting.

Example 15:
Patty and Dave - Flat 6th

Dave and Patty are another perfect example of a flat 6th. While living their busy lives in two countries, they maintain an after school program for the less fortunate children in a small village along the Mexican coast. The time and energy that it consumes from their lives can hardly be noticed, as they consistently seem to be taking on more and more projects that help others. In the busy and complex lives of the flat 2nd and 2nd intervals, making that kind of commitment would be unthinkable. It sometimes appears that only in the flat 3rd, 3rd, and a flat 6th, 6th interval relationship does that level of generosity avail itself. Those are, after all, the intervals of love.

From the outside, flat 6^{ths} appear happy, content, friendly and often in love. For them, one particular trait is unique, the maturity of their worldview. Everyone notices how they express their generous giving and compassionate caring towards those less fortunate.

Inversion to the 3rd

Sometimes the sense of relaxation and lack of tightness in the flat 6th can cause one to feel too complacent. Life can then seem to be void of meaningful challenges. It's almost as though you feel you've been put out to pasture, no longer in the race. The love that was once so hot and steamy now appears to be more careful and deliberate. By inverting to the 3rd, you can spice things up in ways you may have never thought about while in the flat 6th.

In business or social interactions, the competitive edge lies in the 3rd inversion. If both of you are working at the same financial goal, you would have more focused energy, more aggressive vision, more ability for "surgical strikes" than if you remained in the softer, introspective flat 6th. Stay aware of who holds the command at any particular moment. When you do sense the subtle energy of dominance, make a change to the octave (the 3rd) and become more direct, more certain and more deliberate and see how the dynamics change. By developing that new awareness you will be able to consciously partake in the health and success of your personal involvements. Have fun going back and forth between these intervals, it's playful, rewarding and contributes to a successful and lasting relationship.

6th Interval

The beginning of love is to let those we love be perfectly themselves, and not to twist them to fit our own image. Otherwise we love only the reflection of ourselves we find in them

Thomas Merton (The Way of Chuang Tzu, 1965)

Partner Birth Month	Your Birth Month	Partner Birth Month
	January ➡	October
	February ➡	November
	March ➡	December
	April	
	May	
	June	
	July	
	August	
	September	
January ➡	October	
February ➡	November	
March ➡	December	

Staff

6th Interval

C-A

Mildly Dissonant

Characteristics

Pleasurable

Joyful

Earthy

Positive

Saccharine

Redundant

Generous

Musical References

My Bonnie Lies Over the Ocean - Traditional Scottish Folk Song

Louie Louie - The Kingsmen, written by Richard Berry

La Cucaracha - Antonio Bribiesca

It's time again to tighten the tuning peg on that imaginary guitar. Listen as the note being stretched reaches for the next possible interval, that of the 6th. The 6th is the inversion of the flat 3rd. Both intervals contain the same notes. And, many of the attributes of the flat 3rd apply to the 6th. Again, this is an interval of love. It is used in the song "My Bonny Lies Over the Ocean." If you play C, followed by the A above, you'll hear this interval as it sounds in the beginning of this tune.

As you go farther up the interval scale, the distance between the notes or vibratory rates of each person is becoming greater. Like two magnets pulled wider apart, the power of the inherent draw between the two polarities is becoming softer. This decrease in tension between the notes offsets their increasing dissonance. When the earlier intervals were in their primary inversion, before they reached the level of the flat 5th, they were being pulled more forcibly toward one another. Now, with the flat 6th and 6th, even though these intervals are returning to a dissonant state, there is a maturity and graciousness involved.

The musical interval of the flat 3rd, 3rd, flat 6th and 6th share one unique trait: they are the only intervals that tell you what key they are in. The flat 3rd and 6th, because of their unique relationship, tell you that they belong to a distinct set of major keys even though the flat 3rd is a minor interval as opposed to a major interval. For example, the tones C and Eb, a flat 3rd interval, belong to the key of Eb. The 3rd and flat 6th belong to the home key named by the root, or lower tone, of the interval. Hence, the notes C and E belong to the key of C.

What's important to remember is the idea that flat 3rd, 3rd, flat 6th, and 6th are from "home families." They, in essence, have a network of other relationships determined by their key structure.

This network provides the foundation that supports the construction of songs and compositions, especially in many ethnic, pop, country, and children's music.

To put this concept into the context of relationships, we will look at the C, F and G chords in the1963 pop song "Louie, Louie" by Richard Berry. Da-Da-Da, Da-Da, Da-Da-Da, Da-Da etc. The lyrics went "A Lou-eee Lou-I, oh no, me gotta go, yeah, yeah, yeah, yeah...." This song embraced and helped establish the three primary chords of the major scale as they have influenced the popular music of today. Many, many tunes are composed with that chordal progression.

In a 6th relationship you form, like in the song "Louie, Louie," the building blocks of most of the social structures you partake in. The two of you often become of greater importance in the harmonious workings of your social involvement than do those who represent the other intervals. The flat 2nd, 2nd, 4th, 5th and flat 5th all, more or less, look to you for the group structure. The thought of that alone could be daunting, but it could also be energizing to know you possess that much sway over your social relationships.

In music, 6^{ths} perform the duty of creating luscious harmonies that imply romance and full-heartedness. The great folk music of Latin America, called Musica Romantica, is filled with this interval. Listen to the Mexican guitar hero Antonio Bribiesca heartbreakingly play the undeniably corny tune "La Cucaracha". This piece is filled with luscious 6^{ths} and flat 6^{ths}.

Those who find themselves in this interval should be thankful for the ease and generosity inherent in this combination. However, as mentioned in previous chapters, beware of "sameness" which leads to boredom, which in turn leads to apathy and inaction. Think twice before you both dress in those matching Bermuda shorts and Polo Shirts. Use balance when things start to get frayed or tested. One of you needs to choose to be consciously different—perhaps not in agreement for a change—in order to resolve the perpetual challenge of being too connected.

Example 16: Bob and Jane - 6th

A couple I have known for over 40 years, Bob and Jane, present to me what appears to be an idyllic family. They are the most loving and happy two individuals I have known, complete with an extended family that is close and dedicated to one another. To me, they are a remarkable success story. The ease in their relationship is palpable and infectious. From the beginning, I pegged them to be either a 3rd/flat 6th, or flat 3rd/6th. As it turned out during my investigations, I was correct. There are subtle differences between the 3rd/flat 6th and the flat 3rd/6th. The former has a more formal air about the couple and they exude a type of dignity not apparent in the flat 3rd/6th relationship that tends to be more playful and lighthearted in approach.

My two friends created a wonderful interaction based on trust, laughter and balance. At times, they could exhibit the flat 3rd tendency to be too similar but usually would make the proper adjustments, inverting to the 6th, in order to maintain that bit of individuality needed by this interval. Fortunately, this interval relationship is one that is easily reconcilable and not fraught with deep challenges like those found in some of the other intervals.

Inversion to the Flat 3rd

We read above that the 6th is characterized by the words earthy, joyful and positive, as well as the not so "shiny" attributes of saccharine and redundant. The interval of the 6th offers a needed respite of comfort and calm, but often at the expense of appearing stuck in the mud. The 6th relationship, over time, can become so uninteresting and predictable that one's social life whittles down to just the two of you. Everything you do is together, so much so that you have successfully performed the "Vulcan Mind Meld" —you are now one! In order to "pull out," a quick inversion to the flat 3rd is needed where you can experience the attributes of sensuous, romantic, co-operative, caring, and empathetic. In the flat 3rd, you can allow the fun to reign just as it did when you first met. Break out the candles and wine, put a fire in the fireplace and turn out the lights! Your unabashed joy of life will shine through to brighten everyone around you—at work, at school, at play. Then, when you need a break, return to the joyful and earthy 6th, ever mindful of becoming unimaginative and monotonous once again.

Thankfully, no matter how you look at these inversions, they form one of the easiest and happiest of groupings with which to be involved. Both the flat 3rd and the 6th are very comfortable landing spots on the bumpy road of relationships. Feel blessed to be under the wing of these gracious intervals and play those beautiful and romantic harmonies they are so noted for.

Flat 7th Interval

I met a little gypsy in a fortune telling place
I met a little gypsy in a fortune telling place
She read my mind, then she slapped my face

Chris Thile (The Brakeman's Blues, 2006)

Partner Birth Month	Your Birth Month		Partner Birth Month
	January	➡	November
	February	➡	December
	March		
	April		
	May		
	June		
	July		
	August		
	September		
	October		
January ➡	November		
February ➡	December		

Staff

Flat 7th Interval

C-Bb

Dissonant

Characteristics

"Bluesy"

Tense

Expecting

Morose

Yearning

Separated

Chaotic

Musical References

Album "*King of the Delta*" - Robert Johnson

Blue Monk - Thelonius Monk

The beginning of *There's a Place for Us* - Leonard Bernstein

Once again, tune that string on the imaginary guitar just a bit higher. As you slip into the next interval, the flat 7th, you begin to hear the faint strains of the blues. Whoa, babe!

In counterpoint, the interval of the flat 7th creates a dissonant relationship. Great care must constantly be taken to resolve the ever-present tension implied by this interval. It is the inversion of the 2nd though it contains its own unique resonance and power. When used in a musical context it has exceptional ability to punctuate, though not as much as the 7th. This is the interval of the blues! Both jazz and blues make extensive use of the flat 7th to create that distinctive melancholic yearning that people love. Listen to Robert Johnson singing on this archive album titled "King of the Delta Blues Singers" or listen to Thelonius Monk's "Blue Monk."

Like the 2nd, the flat 7th needs space, it needs distance to function. Neither of the tones involved necessarily needs each other to be satisfied and there is not much desire for the flat 7th to continue in any one direction for too long. Hence, this interval, due to the distance the two notes share, is prone to a small, but manageable degree of tension. Yet, just like in the blues, staying on one or two chords for the entire tune is all that is necessary. Simplicity in movement counterbalances the inherent chaos of this interval. Those finding themselves in this relationship more than likely crave independence and freedom. Since the two notes of this interval are farther apart mathematically, too much independence and freedom can cause the relationship to fracture and finally dissolve. This interval creates a feeling of expectancy, suspense, and movement. It is used in the beginning notes of Leonard Bernstein's composition "There's a Place for Us."

When two people find themselves in the flat 7th relationship, it can seem detached or unconnected, although less so than the 2nd. In a family dynamic, this interval can be challenging, though not necessarily confrontational. As lovers, the physical relationship may be the strongest bond they have, as they are both in their heads, on two different planets. In business, generally it's not a good idea to have this interval in partnership as the two parties are at a constant disconnect. In all cases, when they do come together it can look as though they are still not totally in sync; they each do their own thing under the umbrella of their relationship. However, there is a significant chance that each individual party needs and wants this freedom. It is best that each member of this interval has his or her own separate and distinct interests to pursue. This way, conflicts can be avoided, provided they are aware of the demands of the flat 7th, and that a level of harmony - under the shadow of dissonance - can be maintained

Example 17:
Patty & Christopher — Flat 7th

I intimately know several couples that have successfully lived for years in the flat 7th relationship, though at times, the relationships appeared questionable. One couple, Patty and Christopher, whom I have known for many years, suddenly lost their connection. Patty and I talked about this soon after their separation and I gave her the appropriate findings from my study while I was writing this book. I explained that they comprised a 2nd/flat 7th relationship; they inherently were in different mindsets and caught up in their own lives to the seeming neglect of the other. Patty resonated deeply with my words and told me that Christopher, a truly outstanding guy, was so consumed by his photography and other personal things that she consequently felt a void in her life that eventually became overwhelming. Soon after, she realized the potentially uncorrectable pattern she was caught in and separated from Christopher. This caught Christopher off guard and left him surprised and devastated. Happily however, he soon entered into a flat 3rd relationship with a woman and is now experiencing new joy, fun times and hot nights—much to his liking.

In Patty's case, she was embroiled in a mismatched relationship. She was crying out for someone who could recognize and appreciate her for the person she was, someone who could be an active participant in her life. Christopher, the gentleman that he was, was living the perfect flat $7^{th}/2^{nd}$ interval and blindly doing his own thing. There was no doubt that Christopher wanted and enjoyed that level of freedom but, it just didn't work for Patty. She would have been better served moving to a more harmonious interval such as the flat 3rd, 3rd or $4^{th}/5^{th}$.

Even to this day, I believe Christopher felt he was doing everything needed to be a loving and supportive partner. While the interval relationship of a 2nd worked for him, it left Patty in the cold. Had they known about inverting the first month to its octave, they may have been able to rectify and resolve some of the inherent conflict that Patty was experiencing.

Unfortunately, at times, you can reproduce your mismatched relationship, leaving one and replacing it with another of the same pattern. When there are challenging issues with mothers or fathers, people even sometimes duplicate *that* relationship in their future choice of companions. By understanding *Harmonology*, those challenging and recurring relationships can be resolved. You can catch yourself in midthought before you make the same mistake again. Just by knowing what you honestly want and what intervals would serve your desires, you can create the world of your dreams and more ideal relationships.

Inversion to the 2nd

Those that find themselves in the relationship of a flat 7th often experience the feeling of challenge. Mathematically, the vibrations between the two notes (people) are distant and dissonant, manifesting in a slight sense of disconnect. However, by inverting to the 2nd, that disconnect is precisely what drives the relationship forward. It's almost total individual freedom while in a willing contract with another. One strong reason inversion to the 2nd would be desired is to regain that forward propulsion that may be lost in the flat 7th. On one hand, the interval of the 2nd is almost too tight, too much friction. On the other, the flat 7th may be too loose and consequently containing no spark. Moving back and forth often can help to maintain the balance needed for the health of the relationship.

When you hear the blues, it's often sang at a slow, morose and suspenseful pace. The singer milks the basic premise of the piece until, finally, he or she delivers the final resolution. Take a look at the quote at the top of this chapter. These lyrics are typical of early Southern blues. Notice how it states redundant phrases, and makes you wait until the last line for satisfaction. That is often how the flat 7th interval relationship functions. Though it can be a restful place that the 2nd can invert to, it may get bogged down in the overall lack of energy present for people existing in the 7th interval. And, that is exactly when and why you would want to invert to the 2nd, to gain the energy and stimulation contained in that primal interval. Invert and pick up some of the heat that keeps you alive and moving forward. Remember the characteristics of the 2nd: suspense, freedom, open, and eager. After all, isn't that what drew you into the relationship in the first place?

Inversion goes on all the time in your waking hours. Normally, it's of the unconscious type where it happens behind the scrim of life, on automatic pilot. It doesn't matter which interval you are experiencing, you're not alone and we all do it. But, when you become aware of your ability to compress or open at will your spiritual space with someone else, you become master of your destiny. You arrive as the creator of the relationship's outcome. If done with compassion and heart, your friendships and love can flourish and blossom, delivering to you the results of your best dreams. You can finally have the relationships you desire and deserve. All intervals are good, some are just more challenging. But remember, on some level, you choose what degree of intensity or calm you need for your growth.

7th Interval

If I could rearrange the alphabet, I'd put U and I together

Unknown

Partner Birth Month	Your Birth Month	Partner Birth Month
	January ➡	December
	February	
	March	
	April	
	May	
	June	
	July	
	August	
	September	
	October	
	November	
January ➡	December	

Staff	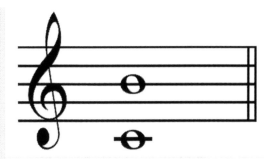 7th Interval C-B Dissonant
Characteristics	Anxious Disruptive Emotionally Heavy Intense Distant Discordant Contentious
Musical References	*Bali Ha'i* – by Richard Rodgers in the musical "South Pacific." Third Phrase in *Superman Theme* – John Williams

7th Interval

This is the point where your imaginary guitar has almost reached its highest tuning. If you tighten the string much more, it will snap! The only place to go from here is to turn that tuning peg until you settle upon the last interval before the octave, the 7th. This time, go to the piano or guitar and together play C and the B found eleven notes higher.

The 7th is the inversion of the flat 2nd, a contentious interval to say the least. Similar to the flat 5th, the flat 2nd and the 7th present the most challenging energy combinations of the entire harmonic spectrum.

Pythagoras showed that these combinations are so high in the ratio numbers as to be ultimately dissonant. There are those who love and crave this combination, and those who fall victim to the intense and challenging vibrational dissonance. Some people need to live in a 7th semi-solitude lifestyle while being in a relationship. The inherent distance between the two parties offers each of them the opportunity to travel solo while within a committed context. If you desire to maintain almost total independence, to be self-directed, to be singular in your nature, the 7th most likely is the relationship interval for you. This structure, as we see in music, exudes a sense of sovereignty. You and your partner both command a freedom to pursue your dreams in the way you see fit and unencumbered by the demands of others. However, unless both partners are in agreement, the challenges could prove to be disastrous.

The 7th creates a feeling of discord and strangeness; it is eerie and ethereal. Listen for it in the forlorn song "Bali Hai" from the musical *South Pacific*. In particular, listen to the main melody after the introduction where you will hear both the 7th and the flat 2nd in consecutive order. The "Theme from Superman," written by John Williams contains a perfect example of the 7th in the third phrase of the melody, just after the introduction, where the brass makes its grand statement.

When you look at the paring of two people in a relationship, each one has their unique vibratory essence. That note—the combined "soundprint" emanating from their unique individual vibrational pattern—will be in resonance with certain types of music and, in particular, individual pieces of music. It's perhaps possible that when one enters into a relationship with another, his or her personal pattern resonates with the pattern of the other. Obviously, the result is the formation of an interval. The chance that they will have similar musical tastes would be dependent upon the degree of harmony or dissonance created by their union. In an article written for *Psychology Today,* Art Markman, PhD and executive editor of *Cognitive Science,* explores how musical preferences may provide information about a person's core values, and that people exhibit musical bonding early in relationship development through the feeling that they share similar values and ideals. (Why Do We Like People Who Like the Music We Do?, 2011) Two people who enjoy the same style songs have a greater chance of creating harmonious interval relationships due to their close vibratory soul resonance. People in a mildly dissonant flat 3rd relationship most likely will have similar preferences in listening than those in the dissonant relationship of a 7th.

It seems logical to assume that one's environment and exposure would have a dominant role in the deciding factors used to form one's tastes; it would be expected that a person born in the countryside would have preferences quite different from someone born in the city. However, this isn't necessarily the case. My wife was raised on a rural farm in Quebec, Canada whereas I spent my formative years in the urban sprawl of San Diego, California. Though worlds apart, we share very similar tastes in music, food, art and travel. It is a product of our interval, a flat 3rd that allows us to find this commonality. How do you musically vibrate with your loved one? Observing the musical tastes of your friends, boss, children and others can teach you a lot. In a journal article titled *Lifestyle correlates of musical preference: 1. Relationships, living arrangements, beliefs, and crime,* Adrian North and David Hargreaves determine that there is a correlation between lifestyle and relationship preferences. (North & Hargreaves, 2007) I suggest that correlations may further be the result of our vibratory patterning and the choices we make, whether conscious or not, based on relationship intervals.

In music, especially 20ᵗʰ century classical and jazz, as well as standards from *The Great American Songbook,* the 7ᵗʰ is utilized with great frequency and aplomb. The character of this interval can be wonderfully pleasing in its dissonance. It creates a beautiful longing and introspective effect on the ear. However, the satisfying result of combining two notes a 7ᵗʰ apart is almost always accomplished by the addition of at least one other note—a mediating note. For example, the beautiful C major 7ᵗʰ chord is defined as having the dissonant combination of the root C and its 7ᵗʰ interval above B, but with the addition of E, the 3ʳᵈ of the chord and most often G, the interval of a 5ᵗʰ. In the image of the major 7ᵗʰ below, the bottom and top notes create our dissonant 7ᵗʰ interval. The notes found between these are the 3ʳᵈ and 5ᵗʰ, from the bottom up.

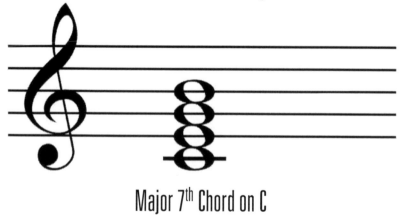

Major 7ᵗʰ Chord on C

For those in the challenging relationship of a 7ᵗʰ, having other influences like children, close friends, business associates, or even a pet intimately involved in their lives is a great way to soften the harsh dissonance produced by this combination of energies.

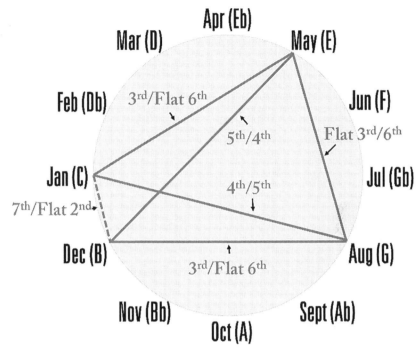

Notice in the above chart that the challenging interval of the 7th/flat 2nd, is easily softened by the addition of the notes E and G. With the added notes, two sets of 3rd/flat 6ths, a flat 3rd/6th, a 4th/5th, and a 5th/4th are formed. These added intervals either are consonant or mildly dissonant intervals, hence softening the dissonance inherent in the 7th/flat 2nd interval.

Inversion to the Flat 2nd

Unlike those who are in a flat 5th interval, those in a 7th relationship can flip-flop between their polarities and maneuver through life's more difficult times. Again, BALANCE is needed to restore the equilibrium when the scales begin to tip. But, alas, along came Mother Nature, who so graciously supplied us with this possibility. What wonderful intelligence nature possesses, that it equipped us with the ability to move smoothly in and out of our inherent relationship challenges. Though we may unknowingly seek to be in a competitive, yet futile relationship, we all also desire a respite, a place of calm from that self-created storm. For each negative there is a positive, for each down there is an up and for each interval, there is an inversion

When the time comes in your 7th relationship to gain intensity, to sharpen the razor's edge, and bring your partnership into focus, it's time to invert to the flat 2nd. Under the influence of the flat 2nd you gain the strength of the shark in "Jaws." But beware, you now possess almost uncontrollable social power. Take care in how you use the potential of this interval, and make yourself aware of the flat 2nd characteristics. When you are done being strong and edgy, invert again to the 7th and take a break, get together and play light-heartedly; become light as a feather in this challenging interval.

Charting Family Dynamics

After a good dinner one can forgive anybody, even one's own relation

Oscar Wilde (A Woman of No Importance, 1894)

In the chapter discussing 7^{ths}, I used a chart to illustrate how the addition of one or two notes (other people) can affect and transmute the energies inherent in an interval relationship. In this chapter, I will show you how to assess any combination of relations, be them blood relatives, co-workers, good friends, or whomever.

The subject of relationships in correlation to musical harmony does not necessarily need to be only a one-on-one with your boss, your spouse or your children. You can analyze your entire family structure. It came to my attention one evening when I was musing over the possibilities of this system and that I might apply it to my own family, my paternal–maternal family, and see what I could learn.

As a preface, my father, whom I'll use as the focus of this particular study, was a challenging and disconnected person. He didn't care much for others nor did he have much affection for the world in general. He was married to my mother, obviously, but there never seemed to be a healthy fit. I had four brothers and a sister, and there unfortunately existed some very deep issues between my oldest brother and my father. I remember my father being an alcoholic—an "Irish tempered" alcoholic. He would have made a fitting character in Frank McCourt's *Angela's Ashes*. Yet, he was a very bright man, though minimally educated. When he was having one of his inebriated moments, he frequently took out his Irish tempered frustrations on my brother Peter through traumatic and brutal physical abuse.

My oldest brother, Peter, was born in February, and my father was born in August. The interval created between February and August is the flat 5th you previously read about. One of the participants in this interval connection needs to be subservient to the more dominant other at all times. As long as my brother attempted to achieve any kind of personal identity, my father beat him back into submission—that's one unfortunate way the flat 5ths can relate at times. The connection does not work if both parties express any sort of equity. One holds the dominance, and the other must give way at all times to that dominance. My father was the assumed alpha-male; when my brother attempted to exert his energy, especially as Peter grew older, my father retaliated with violence.

My father and my brother Joe, who was born in April, were much closer. Joe and my father established a 3rd/flat 6th interval. My father had a lot of hope for Joe; he helped pay for Joe's college education and left him alone to thrive as best he could on his own. Looking at it through the prism of our new understanding, *Harmonology*, and with Joe being a 3rd/flat 6th with my father, I can understand the difference between Joe and my older brother Peter, the flat 5th, and further understand how they interacted with my father.

As for me, I was born in June. I was a 2nd/flat 7th interval with my father. If you remember, 2nd/flat 7th is a very noncommittal, distant and dissonant relationship. Hence, in my family upbringing my father really didn't care one way or another about me, nor what I did, nor if I raised my head above the horizon. I was all but invisible. Those characteristics were all very typical for the parental 2nd interval relationship. He simply could not care less about my presence in the home. After all, interval wise, I was neither a threat nor an asset to him in any way. When the 2nd becomes a flat 7th through inversion, it transforms to the blues interval. In a sense, there were blues between my father and I. Fortunately for me, it was not bad blues whatsoever, nor was it necessarily good for that matter. It was non-committal in its initial stages, but definitely with bluesy overtones.

My next older brother Roger was born in May, and the relationship between my father and him always worked well, they were a flat 3rd/6th. He had no animosity towards Roger and my father allowed him to function as he wished; there were never any complaints from my father. This interval is actually slightly warmer of a relationship than that of Joe and my father. The interval of the 3rd/flat 6th is a little more superficial and stoical than the flat 3rd/6th, which is a bit more colored and nuanced.

When I looked at the *Harmonology* between the three of my siblings and my father, it started making total sense in explaining and sorting out some of the mysterious behavior that happened in our family and, more than likely, it plays out similarly in every family.

My father was also in a dissonant interval-relationship with my mom. She was born in September, and he August, so they were a half step apart, a flat 2nd/7th interval. They did not have a loving relationship that was obvious to the outside observer. My father was distant and removed from my mother, and she appeared to me to have thought little of him. How they stayed married for so long was just, perhaps, a product of the times and of my mother's religious upbringing.

While in that flat 2nd/7th relationship, my father chose to be the dominant one. Chronologically, the first of the two months in the flat 2nd relationship is required to be the subdominant party for the interval relationship to work harmoniously. That is inverting. For instance, if you're born in January and your spouse is born in February, the February spouse wants to hold the dominant role, though that doesn't necessarily mean authoritative or strict. It just means that when issues come to light, the second month needs to be the month that makes the hard choices in order to appease the intense tension between half steps. This allows the first month the possibility to raise an octave so that it helps form a 7th, a much softer interval than a flat 2nd. By making that inversion, there will be a more functional and favorable interval created. The amount of space between the two notes a 7th apart is vastly greater than that of the flat 2nd. So, there is a larger playing field available in order to reconcile some of the contentious issues that arise with this interval combination.

My father, the first month of the parental relationship, refused to give up any of his dominance to my mom. One possible reason was that she was a woman; he grew up in an era where men seldom let women rule. Whatever the reason, he created and maintained through his own misplaced dominance, the peak chaos of the half steps. He blocked the possibility of inverting, thus, dooming any potential of success in their relationship. In a way, they would have been more functional had they been in the interval of the flat 5th.

In review: my father was August, the 8th month, Peter was February, the 2nd month, Roger was May, the 5th month, Joe was April, the 4th month, I was born in June, the 6th month, and my mom was September, the 9th month. Look at the chart below and see how this all plays out.

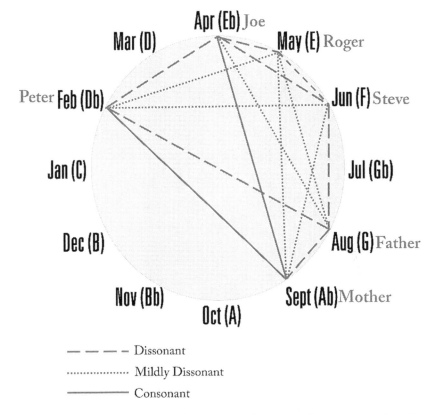

Apr (Eb) Joe
Mar (D)
May (E) Roger
Peter Feb (Db)
Jun (F) Steve
Jan (C)
Jul (Gb)
Dec (B)
Aug (G) Father
Nov (Bb)
Sept (Ab) Mother
Oct (A)

— — — — Dissonant
·············· Mildly Dissonant
——————— Consonant

I had no understanding as to why everything seemed so dysfunctional until I finally charted out my family dynamics using *Harmonology*. Now, I can see that my brothers and I made up a series of flat 2nds/7ths and 2nds/flat 7ths, all dissonant. My father shared mildly dissonant, but good 3rd/flat 6th and flat 3rd/6th relationships with Joe and Roger, a dissonant 2nd/flat 7th with me and a strongly dissonant flat 5th interval with Peter. Had I understood these connections while I was young I could have forgiven and forgotten my family chaos much earlier in life.

If you are in a challenging family dynamic or are the child of a broken family, you may find a resolution by learning to understand the hidden dynamics that were, and possibly still are, at play.

Lolo's Family Dynamics

Besides the two of us, we were blessed to be with Lolo's sons, Dave and Dan, and their partners Christina and Zoe. Lolo was born in March, Christina in November, Zoe in October, Dan in May, Dave in August and I was born in June. In general we got along fluidly. Often, that is not the case, as in the above chart of my birth family. However, as with all families, or all groupings of people, there are issues that arise at times.

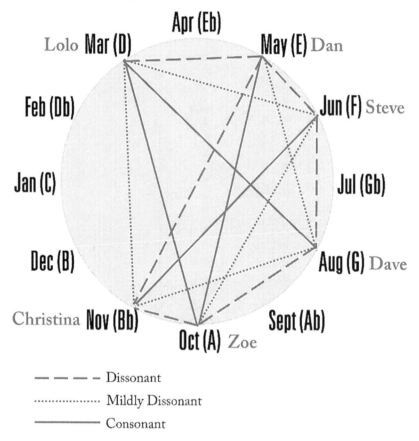

This chart looks scarier than it really is. Don't feel overwhelmed, I will help you understand how it was constructed and then discuss the results that it delivers. You may soon find yourself charting out similar dynamics as you begin to investigate your family dynamics.

I first plotted out each person's birth month. You can see that my wife's nickname Lolo is placed next to the month of March, Dan is placed next to his birth month, May, and so on. Then, going around the circle starting with Lolo, I drew a line and connected each of the people around the circle to each other. Then I placed each interval relationship into a descending color-coded category from consonance to dissonance (see chart below). This allowed me to assess the potentials and identify the areas where special attention and care needs to be placed.

4th/5th — Consonant

- Lolo - Zoe
- Lolo - Dave
- Dan - Zoe
- Steve - Christina

3rd/Flat 6th — Mildly Dissonant

- Lolo - Christina
- Steve - Zoe

Flat 3rd/6th — Mildly Dissonant

- Lolo - Steve
- Dan - Dave
- Dave - Christina

2nd/Flat 7th — Dissonant

- Lolo - Dan
- Steve - Dave
- Dave - Zoe

Flat 2nd/7th — Dissonant

- Dan - Steve
- Zoe - Christina

Flat 5th — Absolute Dissonance

- Dan - Christina

The chart is organized starting with the most consonant relationships and descending to the most dissonant relationships. As a result, we can see that the family will suffer few challenges of any magnitude. There most likely will be the occasional small misunderstandings and disputes among the 4ths/5ths, 3rds/flat 6ths and flat 3rds/6ths, but the resolution will often come easily and quickly, hopefully with no one getting hurt. Where the challenges can be found, are with intervals of the flat 2nd and the flat 5th at the bottom of the column.

Dan and I, and Zoe and Christina form two sets of flat 2nds. The flat 2nd need to honor each other's space. At times, a competition for dominance will arise between these two sets of players. Flat 2nds don't usually give up their power easily; to avoid a clash, both people in the flat 2nd need to be aware of their strength, back off when necessary, invert and seek balance. That interval can create an undercurrent of chaos due to their restless energy and need for self-control.

The next interval harboring potential issues, and perhaps the most contentious ones, is the relationship between Dan and Christina. From what you learned with the family chart above, they are in a flat 5th relationship. That interval is based on dominance and submission. If you go to the chapter on flat 5ths, you will find that the research shows that the female most often plays the dominant role in a heterosexual relationship. That would indicate that Christina holds power over Dan. If that truly were the case, then Dan would continuously need to stay in a passive role in order to ameliorate any contentious issues that may arise in the future. Be assured, this synopsis can never be 100 percent cut in stone. Baggage brought in by either party can sway the manifestations of the characteristics of the intervals but, sensitivity and awareness always will soften any contentious issues.

Also, as in the case of Dan and Christina, if there already is a mutual sensitivity in place where they can recognize and thwart the energy build before it becomes too great and potentially destructive, then they have essentially accomplished what this book set out to show: conscious balance is the answer for strong, long lasting relationships. Please don't forget, all intervals are good and necessary, as long as they work at functioning harmoniously.

Lolo's Birth Family Dynamics

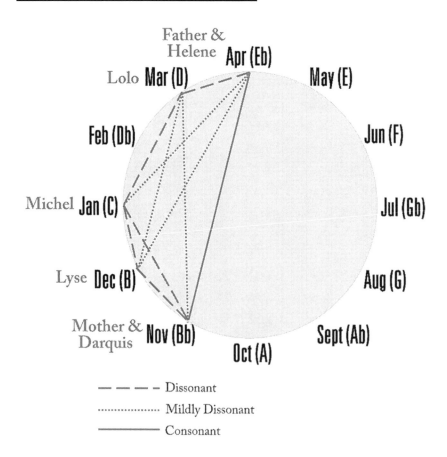

Here is another very exciting and educational family chart. This one is for my wife's birth family. Involved is Lolo's mother and father and her three sisters Helene, Darquise and Lyse, plus her brother Michel.

The first thing to notice in Lolo's birth family is that her mother and father auspiciously form a stable and strong 4th/5th interval. The 4th/5th creates a very firm and supportive pillar, a great foundation for the family. Her sister Darquise is also a 4th/5th to her father, as well as a unison with her mother. She is in sync with her mom and also forms a strong bond with her father. I would guess she had it easy in the family. What could be better than being in total oneness with your mother while having support and strength from your father? Also, notice how the entire family is positioned on one side of the chart, leaving October through May empty. The entire family is rooted in the recessive and cool months of winter.

Next, look at the 3rd/flat 6th intervals formed by Darquise/mother with Lolo. Also, look at the 3rd/flat 6th interval Helene/father (unison) with Lyse. As you read earlier, the 3rd/flat 6th interval is very harmonious and loving. While not as supportive as the 5th/4th found between Darquise/mother with father the 3rd/flat 6th is a very fortuitous interval for relationships, especially between family members.

Lolo and her sister Lyse form a flat 3rd/6th interval. Again, here's a very good and harmonious pairing. Michel and father also form the flat 3rd/6th relationship. So far we have a potential for a harmonious and loving family unit.

Next, look at the periphery of the circle. Here is where we can find a bit more tension and challenge in the family. There are three sets of flat 2nds/7ths. They are between: Lolo/Helene with their father, Lyse/Darquise with their mother, and finally, between Lyse and Michel. While there was a solid foundation formed by mom and dad, we can see there may be a bit of sibling rivalry. That should be no surprise for a family of that size. If you recall the chapter on flat $2^{nd}/7^{th}$, that interval exhibits the characteristics of independence and aloofness. Those who form the flat $2^{nd}/7^{th}$ interval, although they are close family members, function independently and without much connection with their interval partners. There is a chance that communications between these siblings will be minimal in the adult years.

Mother/Darquise combined with Michel form a 2nd/flat 7th. The same is found between Michel and Lolo. With the interval of the 2nd/flat 7th, there is more latitude for reconciliation yet still a degree of aloofness and separation. Chances are that if there were to be family squabbles you most likely would find all their names involved.

Again, chart out your family and gain an insight to the dynamics that was part of your family experience. That information may very well be the "seatbelt" you need to survive in tumultuous family dynamics. I have included blank charts at www.harmonology.mx for you to use. It won't take long before you have mastered this technique and can apply it to all your social connections. Soon, you will be armed with knowledge that most people don't have, knowledge that will allow you to move through life more gracefully, smoothly and successfully using *Harmonology*. You may discover that those who are around you will find you very comfortable to be with after you've applied your newly gained tools.

Baggage

Have no fear of perfection - you'll never reach it

Salvador Dali

As a note for all the intervals, the successes and challenges I describe in this book are predominately taking into account well-adjusted and healthy relationships. When we add into the equation what I call "severe baggage"—child abuse, alcoholism and drug dependency—there is no way to tell how well a relationship will flourish. With the psychology of deep complications, the success of any relationship is questionable

When a person has suffered trauma early in life, it can be like a broken instrument. The ability to create beautiful sounding music with others becomes jeopardized. The intonation is off or the strings are frayed. But, like the damaged instrument, there is always the possibility of repair. Healing can happen, restoring the individual to a level that harmonizes with others to a lesser or greater degree of success.

In a way it is similar to when one of the guitar strings breaks. It can be as simple as replacing the string, what we would call "healing." Often, however, there is no replacement string available and the harmonious relationship erodes and eventually disintegrates.

Baggage

We all carry a set amount of contentious baggage in the way of social conditioning, parental transference and political and religious belief systems. We could call most of that "standard" or "par for the course". For some of us, the baggage becomes a burden and, like the tortoise, we take it around on our backs for the better part of a lifetime. The ultimate nature of the maturing process, going through the crucible of life, is meant to transform many of these questionable, well-intended but misguided attachments into more socially responsible and homogeneous behaviors. An acceptable amount and type of baggage is what forms character and, in turn, society. Belief systems, be they for the better or not, become the guiding force for many, especially those who remain unaware of the beliefs presence and influence.

In this book, I talk about the 12 musical intervals, their propensity for creating consonance or dissonance and their correlation to our personal relationships. In a perfect world, the attributes of the intervals are highly accurate in describing the characteristics of our close interactions in our immediate social network. As telling and illuminating as this process is, it can also be clouded by our baggage, especially when the baggage is of a severe nature. Alcoholism, drug abuse, cultural heritage, sexual addiction, greed, envy and an excessively dysfunctional ego are but a few of the examples that can distort the investigation of any relationship. Someone, for instance, who was married to another—three months apart—formed what we would have considered a harmonious and graceful connection—a flat 3rd. If one of the members of this union brought into the affair a drug or alcohol abuse profile, the chances of creating balance over an extended period of time would be greatly compromised. At times, even a difficult health issue can become the definitive deal breaker in a relationship.

Just being with a person whose ego is distorted, let's say by jealousy, fear or lack of self-esteem, can render the study and understanding of a relationship null. I know of one man in particular who undisputedly loved to cause tension and turmoil with almost everyone he was around, including those nearest to him. From close inspection, his abhorrent behavior appeared to stem from a deep lack of self-respect. His way of socially functioning was to knock down, degrade and humiliate those he cared about so that he, ultimately, was left as the only one standing.

Harold made a flat 3rd with my wife, who was his close friend. Ordinarily, and under healthy circumstances, their relationship should have been a delight. The ease of the flat 3rd, like the 3rd, 4th and 5th makes for a readily created harmonious pairing. However, for Harold, his obtuse social manners negated and neutralized any joy and peace usually found in the flat 3rd interval. Unfortunately, he may live his entire life trapped in that dysfunctional web of self-destruction caused by his paradigm or worldview.

In cases like this, little matters as to what interval you make with someone. It just may be best for the healthier individual to drop the relationship completely and move on to one that holds the promise for success. After all, if it's not a nurturing relationship, it's probably not worth experiencing.

The flat 5th relationship, as we read, is another contentious interval contingent on one of the two parties being decidedly dominant and the other passive at all times. As you saw from my research, it is usually the female, for no observable reason, who is dominant. When the male is dominant in the flat 5th there may be a tendency toward abuse—physical, sexual or psychological—as the energy inherent in this situation can be overwhelmingly strong. If and when the male is in the position of power and bringing with him issues of alcohol or drug abuse, or a psychotic ego, there can exist the potential for grave harm.

Baggage

In the movie "Barfly," based on the life of Charles Bukowski, played by Mickey Rourke, there is a great scene where Barfly picks up a girl at a sleazy tavern and heads back to her apartment. Before entering her room Barfly hears the sound of an impact followed by the scream of a woman, and again the sound of an impact, again followed by the scream of a woman. Rushing to the source of the noise, Barfly knocks down the door right at the moment, caught suspended in time, when a man is preparing to hit a woman he is holding by the throat on the bed. The two people stop what they are doing, turn to Barfly and, in unison, say, "Hey, get out of here! Can't you see we're having fun?" or something to that effect. If that is not an example of an extreme and dysfunctional flat 5th relationship, I don't know what is. In their case, their psychosis (baggage) has taken the interval to its final level of challenging behavior before something agreeable, yet regrettable, happens.

The intent of the scene was obviously a Hollywood exaggeration, but it presents us with an example of the harm baggage can bring into a relationship. I know of many couples that have had potentially harmonious relationships destroyed by one or the other's uncontrollable and unreasonable behavior. The only cure for that is conscious awareness, which is after all the underlying premise of this book. Be consciously aware of your role in your relationship and move toward BALANCE based on the knowledge you gain from understanding intervals and relationships.

Interestingly enough, our baggage may be what actually helps us form our desire to enter into a particular interval relationship. If it were only about living happily ever after, we would all, most likely, choose the flat 3rd or 3rd interval for our partnerships, and what a dull world that would produce. Instead, many of us have needs: to be challenged, to be tested, to be strengthened and, to grow! We are all a part of the Great Symphony of life!

Meditations

It is often said that a person is "caught in their head." In our western culture we depend upon our rational thinking for most of what we encounter in life. While at times that may be good, it can also lead to an erroneous perception of reality. This head-based masculine perspective drives our culture and causes the misunderstandings often encountered in relationships. Reason is a gift, but you cannot successfully reason your way into art or music; you cannot remain present by reasoning and you cannot use reason to fall in love.

With the ability to sense energy you will be able to *feel* whether something or someone is good for you, or not. You will also gain the ability to sense when to step out of a confrontation in which you are not being totally present. Remember, being present means being at one with the moment. That includes not only your external interactions, but also what is going on inside of you

By consistent use of these meditations, as well as others, you will gradually begin to make a permanent move into a new way of being. Over time, your right brain will develop and your heart space will open. Soon, the integration of both hemispheres of the brain will help create a personal world filled with soothing harmony, peace and love. You will find that confrontations come less often and of lesser intensity.

Meditations

These meditations are offered to you as a guide for your personal transformation and to assist in your inversions to healthier relationships. Many of you may be new to the idea of meditation; some may be resistant to either take the time or make the effort. Either way, meditation has lasting and proven benefits well beyond helping you move to a more gracious and softer way of being. Many medical and university studies by experts such as Dr. Herbert Benson, founder of the Mind-Body Medical Institute, (The Relaxation Response, 2000) and Dr. James Austin, a neurophysiologist at the University of Colorado (Zen and the Brain, 1999) have demonstrated exactly how profound and beneficial the act of meditation is.

As quoted from the article "Tune Up with Energy Meditation" some of the benefits include:

• **Increased Immunity**

"Relaxation appears to boost immunity in recovering cancer patients. A study at the Ohio State University found that progressive muscular relaxation, when practiced daily, reduced the risk of breast cancer recurrence. In another study at Ohio State, a month of relaxation exercises boosted natural killer cells in the elderly, giving them a greater resistance to tumors and to viruses

• **Emotional Balance**

"Emotional balance means to be free of all the neurotic behavior that results from the existence of a tortured and traumatized ego. This is very hard to achieve fully, but meditation certainly is the way to cure such neurosis and unhealthy emotional states. As one's consciousness is cleansed of emotionally soaked memories, not only does great freedom abound, but also great balance. As one's responses are no longer colored by the burdens one carries, but are instead true, direct and appropriate.

• **Increased Fertility**

"A study at the University of Western Australia found that women are more likely to conceive during periods when they are relaxed rather than stressed. A study at Trakya University, in Turkey, also found that stress reduces sperm count and motility, suggesting relaxation may also boost male fertility.

• **Relieves Irritable Bowel Syndrome (IBS)**

"When patients suffering from IBS began practicing a relaxation meditation twice daily, their symptoms of bloating, diarrhea and constipation improved significantly. The meditation was so effective the researchers at the State University of New York recommended it as an effective treatment.

• **Lowers Blood Pressure**

"A study at Harvard Medical School found that meditation lowered blood pressure by making the body less responsive to stress hormones, in a similar way to blood pressure lowering medication. Meanwhile, a British Medical Journal report found that patients trained how to relax had significantly lower blood pressure.

• **Anti-Inflammatory**

"Stress leads to inflammation, a state linked to heart disease, arthritis, asthma and skin conditions such as psoriasis, say researchers at Emory University in the US. Relaxation can help prevent and treat such symptoms by switching off the stress response. In this way, one study at McGill University in Canada found that meditation clinically improved the symptoms of psoriasis.

• **Calmness**

"The simple difference between those who meditate and those who do not is that for a meditative mind the thought occurs but is witnessed, while for an ordinary mind, the thought occurs and is the boss. So in both minds, an upsetting thought can occur, but for those who meditate it is just another thought, which is seen as such and is allowed to blossom and die, while in the ordinary mind the thought instigates a storm which rages on and on." (Tune Up with Energy Meditation)

Heart Meditation and Exercise

Lie in a relaxed position for twenty minutes or more. Close your eyes, taking your awareness into your body. Mentally, travel throughout your body releasing any tension as you breathe deeply. Place your attention between the two armpit spaces, and with total concentration "pervade the heart space with a great sense of peace."

Then, forget the rest of your body. Remember the heart area in between the two armpits and in your chest, and feel it filled with wonderful, soothing gold light. When the body is more relaxed, peace automatically will happen in your heart, it will become more silent and harmonious. From there, try to make a contact, a conscious connection with your greater intelligence.

After this meditation and throughout the day, see if you can't access that heart space at will. Once you achieve that new awareness, try moving from head to heart often and observe what happens in your perception. Learn to feel and experience how your entire being shifts to a place of calm, focus and rootedness.

Adapted from: Tantric Sex for Men (Richardson & Richardson, 2010)

Centering Balance Meditation

Begin by bringing your awareness to the center of your chest. So that you can draw your mind into meditation, start to repeat the sound Om, or any sound that you find special or sacred, with each exhalation. You can chant this sound silently at your heart region or out loud, letting the sound originate from your chest, as though you have a voice in your heart. Let the sound vibrate like a deep bell, where your sacred sound ripples in all directions. As you work with the sound, feel that each intonation expands your heart like a great ocean. Stay with the sound and feel that your heart is being cleansed of any unnecessary gripping, tension, or feeling. If a particular emotion arises and starts to overpower the meditation, allow it to be absorbed by your sea of sound. Look underneath, around, and inside that emotion and discover whatever insight may arise from the spaciousness of your inquiry. Gradually, your sacred sound will dissolve into the calm spaciousness of the heart—the great container.

How to Feel and Sense Energy

Take a few deep breaths, relax, clear your mind, and try to sense the energies around you. You may feel a cold, hot or tingly sensation around your body, especially around your palms and fingertips. Move both of your hands in front of your chest with palms facing each other. Your palms should be about a foot away from each other and about a foot away from your chest. Imagine that you're holding a balloon. Try to squish the balloon in a fluidlike motion. As you do this, pay attention to the changes in the atmosphere. Your hands may feel cold, hot or tingly. You may also feel a magnetic force pushing and pulling your hands.

Meditations

For another example, sit comfortably in a straight-backed chair, or stand if you prefer. Maintain your back in a straight line from your sacrum to the top of your head. Feel as though a string from the crown of your head is suspending you. Relax. Now, wait until you feel a warm tingling sensation enter the top of your head. Follow it as it slowly moves down through your body and toward your feet. When it exits your feet and dissolves into the earth, feel the next wave of energy enter your head. Repeat this awareness as you breathe softly, slowly and evenly. Once you can feel and recognize this energetic movement, remember it so that you can recall the sensations and compare them to the energy present in the current situation you find yourself in. By doing so, you will be able to more easily recognize the level of dissonant or consonant energy present in your environment.

Once you understand and master this exercise, try sensing energy in different areas and situations. Subtly, be aware of the energy in your palms while meeting with someone. No one needs to know that your feelers are out. Go outside and 'sense' the vibrational change that is present. Certain situations may make your hands feel colder, hotter or tingly. You may even notice the change in the density of the energy. Over time, you will begin to understand what the energy is personally telling you.

Summary

Color is the keyboard, the eyes are the harmonies, the soul is the piano with many strings. The artist is the hand that plays, touching one key or another, to cause vibrations in the soul

Wassily Kandinsky

Throughout this book, you have continuously tightened that one string on your imaginary guitar—beginning with both strings being equal—until the string reached the point where one was twice as high in pitch as its stable friend. Just like going up the notes, white and black, on the piano keyboard, you have experienced and listened to all the possibilities of sound, from dissonance to consonance and back again. By analogy, you have travelled, through the use of sound, over the landscape of human expression. Along the way, you have stopped to visit each of the 12 dynamics that offer a chance for personal growth.

Your journey could be described in this way:

- You began in pure and simple unison, a reflection in the mirror; you learned of your singular potential and the art of sharing that bounty with someone else. The two of you were the two guitar strings tuned in glorious unison.

Summary

- From that space, needing more freedom to express your separate and personal dreams, you moved on to the flat 2nd. The flat 2nd gave you supreme individuality. No longer was it necessary to share your vision with another. You had your dream, and they had theirs.

- After time allowed for the development of your dreams, you craved the comfort and companionship of another. That urging gave way to the interval relationship of the 2nd. With that interval came empowerment, a sense of being grounded without ties or bonds. You now felt attached to your partner, yet still free to pursue your inner desires.

- Soon, there was a need for more social contact, less intensity and self-concentration. The interval of the flat 3rd presented itself to you and offered a new sanctuary in which to rest. For the first time, you felt the desire to relax into the arms of your lover, taking the time from your previous hectic pace to enjoy the beauty that surrounded you.

- Peace and calm followed your path until it blossomed and matured and gave birth to the interval of the 3rd. With this interval came family, friends and wonderful social interactions. Less time was spent focusing on your personal goals while those close to you were pulled into your primary focus.

- The interval relationship of the 4th provided you, like the 2nd, the freedom to separate from your ties and investigate the many opportunities you held in your hands. The closeness of family and friends remained, but loosened its grip on your ability to expand into new possibilities. You grew stronger as a partnership, rather than as individuals.

- Then came the flat 5ᵗʰ, where your partners no longer held equal balance with you. One of you now needed full reign, as though on a mission. The other had no choice but to give in and be supportive while allowing the stronger to charge on with a full head of steam. It was a unique arrangement like no other, requiring both parties to be in agreement with the energy dynamics, lest the situation become totally out of hand. The flat 5ᵗʰ interval relationship was the place where you gained individual power and strength. There seemed to be little chance in this interval to balance out both the forcefulness and submissiveness.

- When the demand rose, nature supplied the solution by taking you to the next interval. In the interval relationship of the 5ᵗʰ, you experienced the stability and support of your recognizable foundation. Those around you came to rely upon your convictions and visions. Life was good. Balance was finally achieved, and both of you were functioning on equal terms. However, sustained stability is only suitable for so long until a challenge is created.

- Then, the two individuals separate somewhat and move toward the interval of the flat 6ᵗʰ. With the interval relationship of the flat 6ᵗʰ, you saw a reminder of the dynamics of the 3ʳᵈ. Social interactions were again prime; yet there was a maturing beyond the 3ʳᵈ interval that provided for grace and insight. You found it to be a comfortable and loving environment, maintained with ease and joyousness.

- As the two of you separated even more, looking for your lost individuality, the two of you fell into the interval relationship of the 6ᵗʰ. In the interval relationship of the 6ᵗʰ, you again found your lost identities, held on to your social connections while you still lovingly nurtured your family and friends. A new world opened up to you, one in which you explored those dreams you put aside when you entered the earlier relationships.

- Soon, with even more separation from your partner, you once again moved toward your personal goals and visions. The path led to the interval of the blues. The interval relationship of the flat 7th came with a sense of being grounded without ties or bonds. Again, you faced a similar circumstance of being freed from ties to your partner. While you spent more energy on your visions and quests, you relied less upon the interaction with and support of your soul mate. That was fine, since your soul mate was also feeling the freedom and using it, similar to you, to realize their personal dreams.

- As you moved farther into your private world, the last interval, the 7th offering you the chance to be on your own while in union with your partner. In this interval, you spent less time relating and more time pursuing your goals and interests. Your partner found no issue with that interplay as they were also following their own personal bliss.

- And finally, the cycle returned to the octave, the expanded inversion of the unison.

Applying the music intervals to your combined birth months is like watching a flower open. At first, there seems to be a struggle, followed then by a wonderful scent, color and beauty. Finally, it returned to the beginning, but this time filled with knowledge, wisdom and grace, maturity and sensitivity. Perhaps, if you return to participate in life again, you may have the chance to experience all the inversions and intervals. It very well may be the wheel of life spelled out through music and relationships.

Appendix

Participants	Birth Month											
	Jan C	Feb Db	Mar D	Apr Eb	May E	June F	July Gb	Aug G	Sept Ab	Oct A	Nov Bb	Dec B
Unison												
Jesse											●	
Sally											●	
Rob					●							
Helena					●							
Flat 2nd/7th												
Jack							●					
Ann								●				
Allen				●								
Naomi					●							
Jeff								●				
Sheryl							●					
Craig							●					
Betty						●						

Participants	Birth Month											
	Jan C	Feb Db	Mar D	Apr Eb	May E	June F	July Gb	Aug G	Sept Ab	Oct A	Nov Bb	Dec B
2nd/Flat 7th												
Willy									●			
Nancy							●					
Lea									●			
Gunnar							●					
Harriet									●			
Claude											●	
Joe		●										
Wendy				●								
Bob							●					
Lea									●			
Oliver												●
Oliver's Cat										●		
Patty										●		
Christopher												●
Flat 3rd/6th												
Cat #1				●								
Cat #2							●					
Steve						●						
Lolo			●									
Dave									●			
Glenda						●						
Dave								●				
Christy											●	
Steve									●			
Natalie												●
Bob		●										
Jane										●		
Stephen						●						
Sharon									●			

Appendix

Participants	Birth Month											
	Jan C	Feb Db	Mar D	Apr Eb	May E	June F	July Gb	Aug G	Sept Ab	Oct A	Nov Bb	Dec B
3rd/Flat 6th												
James						●						
Christina										●		
Jan										●		
Jim		●										
Patty										●		
Dave						●						
Charmaine								●				
Anonymous				●								
Victor	●											
Joanna									●			
Mike									●			
Monique	●											
Adriana										●		
Eddie						●						
Ara								●				
Tim					●							
Wendy			●									
Ben											●	
Patty							●					
Doug												●
Carl			●									
Jay										●		
4th/5th												
Adriana										●		
Daughter					●							
Brian									●			
Claudia		●										
Jana										●		
Mijo					●							

Participants	Birth Month											
	Jan C	Feb Db	Mar D	Apr Eb	May E	June F	July Gb	Aug G	Sept Ab	Oct A	Nov Bb	Dec B
Karla										●		
Ted			●									
Annie					●							
Aaron												●
Steve			●									
Audry										●		
Jim		●										
Mika							●					
Tom						●						
Tom's Wife											●	
Rob						●						
Sharon	●											
Simone										●		
Girlfriend			●									
Flat 5th												
Linette						●						
Paul												●
Vetta						●						
Husband												●
Judy								●				
Lawrence		●										
Carol	●											
David							●					
Alice												●
Francisco							●					
Lin												●
Mark							●					

Works Cited

Austin, J. (1999). *Zen and the Brain*. MIT Press.

Benson, H. (2000). *The Relaxation Response*. New York: HarperCollins.

Bernstein, L. (1976). *The Unanswered Questions: Six Talks at Harvard*. Cambridge, Massachusetts: Harvard University Press.

Campbell, J. (1988). *The Power of Myth*. New York: Doubleday.

Costa, M., Bitti, P. E., & Bonfiglioli, L. (2000). Psychological Connotations of Harmonic Musical Intervals. *Psychology of Music, 28*(1), 4-22.

Curtis, M. E., & Bharucha, J. J. (2010). The Minor Third Communicates Sadness in Speech, Mirroring Its Use in Music. *Emotion, 10*(3), 335-348.

Evans, B., & Hall, C. (1971). Two Lonely People [Recorded by B. Evans]. On *The Bill Evans Album*. New York City, New York, United States of America: H. Keane.

Jabr, F. (2010, June 17). Music and speech share a code for communicating sadness in the minor third. *Scientific American*. Retrieved from http://blogs.scientificamerican.com/observations/2010/06/17/music-and-speech-share-a-code-for-c-2010-06-17/

Jung, C. (2005). *Modern Man in Search of a Soul*. Oxon: Routledge.

Kaku, D. M. (2012, December 29). *Dr. Kaku's Universe - Math is the Mind of God*. Retrieved from bigthink.com:

http://bcove.me/ogiicdx0

Markman, A. (2011, August 9). Why Do We Like People Who Like the Music We Do? *Psychology Today*. Retrieved from http://www.psychologytoday.com/blog/ulterior-motives/201108/why-do-we-people-who-the-music-we-do

Merton, T. (1965). *The Way of Chuang Tzu*. New York: New Directions.

North, A. C., & Hargreaves, D. J. (2007). Lifestyle correlates of musical preference: 1. Relationships, living arrangements, beliefs, and crime. *Psychology of Music, 35*(1), 58-87.

Richardson, D., & Richardson, M. (2010). *Tantric Sex for Men.* Inner Traditions/Bear & Co.

Shepherd, P. (2013, April). Out of Our Heads. (A. Buchbinder, Interviewer) The Sun.

Sudo, P. T. (1998). *Zen Guitar.* New York: Simon & Schuster.

Tchaikovsky, M. (1906). *The Life and Letters of Peter Ilich Tchaikovsky.* (R. Newmarch, Trans.) London: John Lane.

Thile, C. (2006). The Brakeman's Blues [Recorded by C. Thile]. On *How to Grow a Woman from the Ground.* Sugar Hill Records.

Tomes, R. (n.d.). *Cycles in the Universe.* Retrieved from http://ray.tomes.biz/

Towler, S. (2014). *The Tao of Intimacy and Ecstasy.* Boulder: Sounds True.

Unknown. (2011, June 4). *Benefits of Meditation.* Retrieved from Meditation Mojo: http://www.meditationmojo.com/meditation-articles/introduction-to-meditation/benefits-of-meditation

Unknown. (n.d.). *The Benefits of Relaxation.* Retrieved from My Relax: http://www.myrelax.org/benefitsrelaxmeditation.htm

Unknown. (n.d.). *Tune Up with Energy Meditation.* Retrieved from

Works Cited

Energy Clinic: http://energyclinic.ca/tune-up-energy-meditation/

Wilde, O. (1894). *A Woman of No Importance.* London.

Wilhelm, R. (1967). *The I Ching or Book of Changes.* (C. F. Baynes, Trans.) New Jersey: Princeton University Press.

Wooten, V. (2008). *The Music Lesson.* New York: The Berkley Publishing Group.

About the Author

Stephen John O'Connor started his musical career as a child prodigy. Being a gifted and visionary jazz guitarist and composer, he won the prestigious Downbeat Magazine full scholarship to the Berklee College of Music in Boston. Throughout his early years in the music industry, Stephen was blessed with insights and guidance through dreams, intuition and visions, leading him to a high level of achievement. Amongst his notable commissions and assignments were movie scores, symphony contracts, composing for Universal Studios, Warner Bros., Sea World, The Republic of China, NASA Space and Rocket Center, and The Discovery Channel.

His spiritual contact also brought him on a deep search for meaning. His first book *Counterpoint to Reality*, (available on amazon as both an e-book and print) is a memoir of that quest and describes many of the fascinating and almost unbelievable adventures behind the curtain of reality.

Finally, both his spiritual quest and his musical expertise have joined together in *Harmonology*, to create a totally new and visionary concept that links the laws of music with the laws of nature and our relationships. This insightful book ties together into one worldview the various ideas of vibrating bodies and the basic homogeneous nature of life.

Stephen now spends his time between Quebec, Canada and the Nayarit Coast of Mexico.

You can provide feedback at www.harmonology.mx or on Stephen's Twitter account @harmonology1. Stephen also encourages you to leave a review on Amazon.com.

Also By Stephen O'Connor

Available online at www.amazon.com or www.harmonology.mx

Made in the USA
Charleston, SC
28 November 2014